PRAISE FOR *THE RECRUIT'S PLAYBOOK*

"*The Recruit's Playbook* encompasses everything I wish I had known as a high school student-athlete with dreams of playing at the next level, and in a not-so-stellar situation. Every football prospect should be armed with Coach Hart's guide."

    —Rashad Jennings, *New York Times* bestselling author, former NFL running back, and *Dancing with the Stars* season 24 champion

"Want to play college football and don't know where to start in the football recruitment process? Save yourself some time and read this book! Part football industry insider tips, part personal development pointers, *The Recruit's Playbook* is chock-full of timely and practical ways to jumpstart your journey. Man, I wish I had this guide when I was in high school, figuring things out during my own recruitment process. Coach Hart's guide delivers!"

    —Maurice Jones Drew, three-time Pro Bowl running back, two-time All-Pro running back, and current NFL network analyst

"Players and parents: if the intricacies of the football recruitment process baffle you, Coach Hart does a tremendous job here of shedding some serious light. Through the transparency of his own journey, players can come away with the tools they need to take charge and capitalize. It's a football recruitment tell-all, and highly recommended reading."

    —Mark Freeman, head football coach and eight-time state champion, Thompson High School (Alabama)

"If you want the full scope of the recruiting process from a coach's perspective, speaking directly to t͟ for you. I am recommending *The* ͟ another on the market that captuɪ

recruiting process while also being fully transparent, with added personal anecdotes included. Coach Hart truly takes a deep dive into the highs and lows of his own journey, as he breaks down the road that lies ahead for college football prospects in a truly relatable way. It's a must read."

 —Doug Belk, associate head coach/defensive coordinator, University of Houston

"Athletes, here's a book you'll want to read. *The Recruit's Playbook* is the perfect primer for anyone interested in the high school football recruitment process. From players and parents, to coaches and educational stakeholders—for all of us that are directly impacted by the successful recruitment of high school football athletes, Coach Hart lays it all out plainly, takes out the guesswork, and equips you with a new way of viewing and navigating your recruiting journey. *The Recruit's Playbook* answers the pertinent questions that coaches are asked every single day. 'It's chess, not checkers,' and trust me, you'll want to add this one to your booklist."

 —Blake Anderson, head football coach, Utah State University

"If you care deeply about playing college football, want the answers to the most pressing (and sometimes overlooked) questions, and need a structured to-do list for each grade of high school to help with your recruitment, then put *The Recruit's Playbook* on your required-reading list. Coach Hart offers straight talk and presents a strong plan of attack for high school athletes."

 —Joe Cauthen, defensive coordinator, University at Buffalo

"Thank you to Coach Larry Hart, my former teammate, for taking the time to educate potential recruits, parents, and even coaches about what the recruiting world holds in *The Recruit's Playbook*. Coach Hart dives into the tough questions that oftentimes get overlooked in one of the biggest decisions of a young student-athlete's life. [This book facilitates] healthy conversations between parents and coaches that can help a young student-athlete make the decision for what they are seeking in what can be the most anxious and life-changing of times. *The Recruit's Playbook* covers everything you need to know to prepare and be comfortable about the decisions that are in front you. After reading this book, one will have the confidence to make the best choice and be ready to succeed knowing they have already received the most valuable information there is."

—Kirk Morrison, NFL veteran, ESPN broadcaster/radio host, and SiriusXM NFL host/analyst

"*The Recruit's Playbook* is a must read for players, parents, and high school coaches across the globe. This is a book that will revolutionize the world of recruiting, while empowering and equipping readers with the necessary and valuable insights that will take you behind the scenes and uncover the mysteries of recruiting. This long-awaited masterpiece written by Coach Larry Hart will give you the necessary tools to not only win, but dominate the recruiting process."

—Spencer Ruggs Jr., president of Covenant Sports Academy

"It is an honor to endorse Larry Hart as a rookie author, having selected him in the fifth round of the 2010 NFL Draft out of University of Central Arkansas. He was a highly productive undersized edge rusher who earned his way into an NFL opportunity via the long road. I am a firm believer that character is a player's greatest talent and Larry was a selfless, reliable, and trustworthy teammate.

"This book is an enjoyable and informative read for anyone desiring to learn more about the college recruiting process. The underpinning of Larry's recommendations will resonate with you because they come from his own personal experiences and sheer perseverance. And the content Larry provides in his practical guide, as well as the individual exercises he shares, will benefit those striving to gain exposure and understanding of what it takes to set themselves up for success as a prospective student-athlete."

—Gene Smith, former general manager of the
   Jacksonville Jaguars

"I was honored to share the field and locker room with Larry Hart for two years in the National Football League. Larry's journey from playing at a DI-AA (FCS) school to the NFL is a testament to what it takes to defy the odds and create a better life for yourself not only professionally, but also personally. His achievements didn't happen by chance or luck. Larry was able to forge his path through hard work, dedication, and mindset, all while, most importantly, staying true to himself."

—Austen Lane, ESPN radio host and former NFL player

"Larry Hart has put together a tremendous resource for potential football recruits and their parents in his book *The Recruit's Playbook*. He answers all of the questions that come up at each stage of the recruiting process. So many potential recruits "don't make the play" because they overlook one or more of the scenarios that Coach Hart covers in his book. If you have questions about NCAA eligibility, recruiting dead periods, quiet periods, contact periods, recruiting services, prospect camps or when and how to start the recruiting process you simply must get Coach Hart's book. This is the book to have in order to navigate the recruiting landscape in a post Covid world!"

—Steve Campbell, former FBS head coach, 2x national
   champion (JUCO and D2)

THE RECRUIT'S PLAYBOOK

THE RECRUIT'S PLAYBOOK

A 4-Year Guide
to College Football Recruitment
for High School Athletes

COACH LARRY HART

TURNER

PUBLISHING COMPANY

Turner Publishing Company
Nashville, Tennessee
www.turnerpublishing.com

The Recruit's Playbook: A 4-Year Guide to College Football Recruitment for High School Athletes

Cover/Interior Design: Morgane Leoni
Cover Photos: © digitalskillet1 / stock.adobe.com
Author Photo: © Jules & Co. Consulting / julesconsults.com

Library of Congress Cataloging-in-Publication number: 2021938420
ISBN: (print) 78-1-64250-610-5, (ebook) 978-1-64250-611-2
BISAC category code YAN049000 YOUNG ADULT NONFICTION / School & Education

Printed in the United States of America

To my lovely wife, Juliet, who is the beauty and brains behind the operation. You bring excitement into my life and inspire me in every way imaginable. To Kim, the best mother-in-law to ever do it, my true friend Ruggs, who encouraged me to write, my family, and all of the coaches who have made an impact on my life—

You are appreciated.
#NoGutsNoGlory

TABLE OF CONTENTS

Foreword — 11

Start Here (X): **An Introduction** — 13

Part I: Pre-Game—O — 19

Chapter 1: **Know Your "Why" (X)** — 20

Chapter 2: **Separate Yourself (O)** — 34

Chapter 3: **One Size Does Not Fit All (X)** — 54

Chapter 4: **It's a Mind Game (O)** — 60

Chapter 5: **Football Divisions (X)** — 69

Chapter 6: **Star Ratings & Recruiting Tiers (O)** — 79

Part II: Kick-Off—X — 85

Chapter 7: **1st & 10—Ninth Grade (O)** — 86

Chapter 8: **2nd Down—Tenth Grade (X)** — 99

Chapter 9: **3rd & Short—Eleventh Grade (O)** — 107

Chapter 10: **RedZone—Twelfth Grade (X)** — 132

Part III: Post-Game / Overtime—O — 140

Chapter 11: **Next Play (X)** — 141

Chapter 12: **No Excuses (O)** — 147

Post-Reading Questions — 151

Post-Reading Activities — 152

Acknowledgements — 156

About the Author — 157

FOREWORD

I am truly honored to introduce debut author Coach Larry Hart and the sound advice and key ideas he presents in *The Recruit's Playbook: A 4-Year Guide to College Football Recruitment for High School Athletes*. As a fellow veteran of the collegiate football recruiting process and having learned many things the hard way, when Larry told me about his playbook, I immediately recognized the need and was intrigued.

Early in my NFL career, I had the pleasure of being Larry's teammate while playing with the Jacksonville Jaguars. I got to know Larry as a comrade in between meetings and learned more about his story and character during our cold tub rehab sessions and our locker room and cafeteria talks. We also attended Celebration Church of Jacksonville during our time as Jaguars. Coach Hart and I shared parallel paths in being late-round draft picks with setbacks and stacked odds, as well as not having the most desirable childhood at times. In my book *The If in Life,* I share my personal journey and discuss how to get off the sidelines of life and get into the game by encouraging readers to follow their dreams. *The Recruit's Playbook* includes Larry's personal narrative of challenges and shortcomings to encourage teens to reach their goal of playing Division I football as he did. In the same manner that my life story *The If in Life* uses inspiration to motivate readers, *The Recruit's Playbook* provides its readers a detailed map and lays out a solid plan and strategy for the high school athlete's trek through the complex recruitment process. There are many questions asked when it comes to American football recruitment that oftentimes leave prospects and parents baffled. Larry does a tremendous job of answering those pressing questions that players need answered most and may not even know to ask. This book encompasses everything I wish I had known as a high school student-athlete in a not-so stellar situation with dreams of playing at the next level. Every football prospect should be armed with Coach Hart's guide.

Obviously, football is a huge part of American culture, and this guide is much needed. As Coach Hart and I are both former student-athletes, over the years we were constantly surrounded by peers and teammates with the talent to play Division I football, but many didn't quite have the know-how to best navigate the playing field or the tools to help them seize the opportunity appropriately. Larry has the remedy for this issue and fills a need successfully. This guide evens the playing field for kids from any and all walks of life and backgrounds.

To whom much is given, much is required. Much like myself, Larry has ventured a long way from his humble beginnings and is now giving back and expanding his reach. He definitely possesses the firsthand experience to provide a wealth of insight which he clearly executes in his book, *The Recruit's Playbook*. Larry gives young athletes the ability to take control of their own destiny, and he sets them on a course to pursue their dreams of playing at the next level.

I will take the ideas presented in this powerful tool and share them with the young athletes I come across who are in search of the how-tos, pointed advice, football education, and a customizable, grade-level-specific plan for recruitment. *The Recruit's Playbook* will no doubt help many prospects get off the sidelines and into the game.

—**Rashad Jennings**, *New York Times* bestselling author, former NFL running back, *Dancing with The Stars* Season 24 Mirrorball Champion

AN INTRODUCTION

You're welcome.

If I would have had a mere fraction of the information in *The Recruit's Playbook* while I was in high school (or the wherewithal to research), I would have been a Division I football qualifier...but I didn't and I wasn't. Furthermore, my recruitment out of high school was nonexistent.

As a result, and with hindsight being 20/20, I've compiled and purged all that I have learned along the way to offer you a fool-proof assist to fill the gaps and blind spots that I missed. The purpose of this book coincides with my passion, which is to pour into young student-athletes and provide them the tools they need to be successful on and off the field.

The Recruit's Playbook is a guide for student-athletes to successfully navigate the recruiting process. I believe in teaching student-athletes how to fish:

> **"IF YOU GIVE A MAN A FISH, YOU FEED HIM FOR A DAY. IF YOU TEACH A MAN TO FISH, YOU FEED HIM FOR A LIFETIME."**

As a coach and educator, I want to provide the student-athletes with the ability to eventually take care of (and fish for) themselves. When you are preparing to go off to college, whether you (the student-athlete) realize it or not, you are transitioning and preparing for adulthood. Thus, it is critical to begin developing the skills of being a problem solver and self-starter.

I began my football journey at the age of twelve, and I am currently thirty-three years old. Football has been part of my life for quite some time. During my football journey, there have been a lot of ups and downs along the way. In *The Recruit's Playbook*, we talk about everything from me barely being recruited out of high school to being named MVP of my junior college team, going on to have several scholarship offers coming out of junior college, and playing Division I and professional football.

Now, as a college football coach at the University of Houston, I can look back on the road I have traveled thus far, riddled with the best and worst of times, to appreciate the lessons and experiences that I will continue to build upon, grow from, and take with me for the rest of my life. Change, evolution, and adaptation are good. In the last ten years, the longest I have lived in the same spot was three years. Every two and a half years, I relocate to a different city. Needless to say, I have been pushed out of my comfort zone a time or two.

I am challenging you, the student-athlete, to gain the mindset to embrace discomfort. It is comparable to athletes lifting weights; there is a certain amount of pain associated with weight training. When you experience pain or discomfort, that doesn't mean you stop. Actually, it is the exact opposite. You push through the discomfort to get results. When you push through the pain and continue lifting in spite of the resistance, you get stronger.

For those with the resources, it can be easy to go to a parent or loved one and ask them to do the work for you. What is challenging is learning to find a way for yourself. Yes, it is tough and uncomfortable. But here is a secret: nothing grows while you are in your comfort zone. If you truly want to do something special with your life, it's going to take you being uncomfortable from time to time.

At some point in time, you will experience loss. However, that does not make you a loser. Just because you lose a battle doesn't mean you have lost the war. It is extremely important to master the ability of bouncing back. While things might not go your way, understand that it's all a part of life. There is no need to hit the panic button and get into a negative mindset. Learn to pivot, learn, adjust, and move on. I am not speaking to you based on what I think; I am speaking from what I know. #NoGutsNoGlory

So with all that being said, I highly suggest taking control of your future in high school prior to getting into college. Ask yourself: why not start learning to ask the right questions and being proactive about utilizing the resources that are available to you? Trust me, *time waits for no man*. The time to grow and develop is now.

When student-athletes read these digestible bites of information, I strongly believe it will catapult them down a path to crushing the recruitment process and ultimately achieving the goal of playing collegiate football. What is also great about this information is that these skills will translate into many other areas of life and will potentially give you a leg up on your competition.

As a college football coach, I enjoy being a resource for young men to help them get to where they need to be as players and successful individuals. I put a large emphasis on teaching players to take ownership of their lives. When student-athletes arrive on campus, coaches, players, and everyone involved will need to understand the magnitude of what's at stake. The next four years of your life will set the tone for the next forty.

This guide will provide you, the student-athlete, with the Xs and Os needed to become better self-advocates, with the tools to take on a more active role in your academic goal setting, and ultimately with the ability to execute your plan and become a more successful student. It is extremely important for you to understand that typically at this stage of life, no one is more interested in your life and whether or not you become a success story than *you*.

The dreaded "woulda, coulda, shouldas"...we have all heard them and I have fallen back on them myself. So in providing a measurable, attainable, and deadline-driven plan of attack, student opportunities for success can be realized and their need for excuses diminished.

While I have used my fair share of woulda, coulda, and shouldas, as I suggested earlier, I learned and grew from my losses and mistakes. The only opportunity I had coming out of high school was a 50 percent offer to play junior college football in Mississippi. This is likely due to the fact that my grades were poor and I did not take the ACT until my last semester of high school. I was also around five feet eleven inches to six feet tall. Some things are in your control (grades) and some are not (height). Control the controllables.

Truth be told, I almost gave up on my dream of playing college football. Thankfully, I did not cancel my dreams as it is so easy to get down, defeated, and give up—much easier than standing firm and fighting the giants in our lives. Instead, I used the lessons I am sharing with you to help propel me to a number of successes: an All-American and a Conference Defensive Player of the Year in college, as well as a finalist for the Buck Buchanan National Player of the

Year. Eventually, I was selected in the fifth round by the Jacksonville Jaguars in the 2010 NFL Draft. We will discuss more of my personal story in the coming chapters, but here's the key takeaway: stand firm, roll with the punches, and always keep fighting.

Although I was extremely blessed during my football career, while I was being recruited out of junior college, I wanted to play for a bigger program. That offer never came, yet I was able to fulfill a dream of playing in the NFL. These experiences have given me a very unique perspective. I went from playing in the mud versus Northeast Community College in late October, to playing for a division title versus Peyton Manning and the Indianapolis Colts.

The path I had to take was tough, but it gave me valuable lessons that have helped shape me into the individual I am today. I encourage you to do the same. Use the difficult times to become stronger and wiser. These unique (and often painful) experiences have enabled and afforded me the opportunity to be in a position to provide you and other future student-athletes the keys to being successful.

I would like to take the time to note that success is a very subjective term. A lot of student-athletes would argue that success is making it to the NFL. Social media shows you OBJ dancing in the endzone after a big touchdown catch or Von Miller turning the corner for a big sack on the quarterback. This leads many of us to compare our lives against or measure success based on those outcomes. Instead, I encourage you to attempt to adapt tunnel vision: exclude outside factors or the paths of others and insert your own measures of success.

I once coached a player by the name of Doug. Doug came from a difficult background, and he was undersized much like I was. He was also a walk-on (a non-scholarship player) to the team. Doug always worked hard in practice and he always carried a great attitude. He never complained; he just showed up to work every day. I remember him telling me that he'd had conversations with people who basically told him that he was not good enough to play Division I college football. He, in turn, ignored the naysayers and focused on his dream.

During Doug's second season, he not only earned playing time and got into games, but he was also a player the coaches depended on in meaningful game snaps. Doug started on two of the four major special team units and was on second team defense. This basically means he was the first to rotate in when the starter came out of the game. Although Doug was undersized, he made up for it with intelligence and tenacity.

Along with his football play, Doug also performed in the classroom. I'm certain if anyone were to ask Doug whether or not he was successful, he would say he was. He is well on his way to earning a full-ride scholarship and getting a college degree. Success is subjective and should be treated as such—I would be careful about taking a cookie-cutter approach to it. Instead, focus on being the best version of yourself and working your tail off!

This guide is meant to be shared. Once you've followed *The Recruit's Playbook* and reached the goals presented here, be sure to pay it forward and pass it on to the next recruit.

Finally, the information presented here offers a sure "win-win" for the interests of students, parents, coaches, and educational stakeholders alike.

Cheers to your success, and let's get to work!

—Coach Hart

Part I

PRE-GAME—O

CHAPTER 1
KNOW YOUR "WHY" (X)

Ask yourself: Am I sure I want to go through the recruiting process and play football at the next level? Giving an honest answer to this question is critical, and to do so...

First, know your "why." Do you love football, or do your parents love it for you? Collegiate athletics can offer you an opportunity for a free-ish education, plus benefits. You'll travel, get free gear, be well taken care of, and possibly attend four years of school with little to no money ever leaving your parents' pockets. From a parent's perspective, what's not to love? But can *you* honestly say the same? While your parents may love the game for you, they cannot compete or complete the daily grind that comes along with it. You must stand on your own two feet. Are you chasing status and attention, rather than reality? Are you simply going with the crowd and/or chasing clout? Be honest and true in your answer.

I'm not one to bash social media. I actually enjoy it and believe that it has some really positive attributes. However, social media can unintentionally give the wrong impressions to young student-athletes. For example, when you're scrolling through Instagram or Twitter, you only see highlights. You only see James Harden hit the crossover step-back three-pointer (often with a travel). You only see JuJu catch a one-handed touchdown and start dancing. Let's not forget about your peers posting videos or photos of themselves competing at some kind of seven-on-seven tournament. Shortly after the tournament, all you see on Instagram are your buddies, straight flexin'. But what does this all mean? Are you able to look beyond what is being posted to see what is not?

During my junior year of high school, my head coach asked me to join the powerlifting team. Powerlifting is a sport where student-athletes lift as much weight as possible. Usually there are three lifts, and at competitions the judges will take how much weight you lift on each of the three lifts, then combine the total. The three lifts were squat, bench, and deadlift. While I was a younger high school player, I used to be so amazed watching the older guys lift super heavy weights, especially when it came to max out day.

The guys on the powerlifting team would usually train for about three to four weeks straight. Max out day was an opportunity for the players to see how much improvement they had made. Maxing out is basically the player lifting the maximum amount of weight he or she can—pushing themselves as close to their limit as possible. During max out day, everybody on the team would gather around each player as they attempted their personal best. I'd also like to mention that the powerlifting team would usually do their workouts in a separate room where no one else would see them.

Obviously, I was very excited to have the opportunity to join the team—when I was a freshman, I saw how strong those individuals were! My idea was to use powerlifting to get stronger and more explosive, and to leverage these benefits on the football field as well. "Let's go!" This excitement quickly faded and turned into harsh realism when I reached the first squat day. On that day, our head coach introduced us to two sets of twenty-five reps. This means I had to squat a certain weight twenty-five times, for two rounds. This brought the total reps to a cool fifty. *Ouch!*

It finally dawned on me that these guys did not just get strong by chance. They got stronger because they were working really hard—freakishly hard. As a freshman, I just remember seeing everyone pumped up at max out day, loving the amazing outcomes and fruits of their labor. Before joining the team, I never actually witnessed the day in, day out strict grind and work ethic of those individuals. Needless to say, after my first squat workout, instead of celebrating and posting on social media, I spent my time regurgitating my lunch from earlier in the day. There were many days where it was difficult to sit or stand due to the severe soreness in my legs. I noticed that those factors (and the actual blood, sweat, and tears) were missing from the highlight reel. I grew from the initial anguish and discomfort as a freshman to become a state powerlifting champion by my junior year, and was featured by various news outlets.

My high school powerlifting journey further cemented the concept that you have to be willing to pay the price in order to achieve your goals. And as planned, the strength and explosiveness afforded to me by adding powerlifting to my skillset did pay off tremendously, but not before I worked for it. When you see athletes making big plays in a game or a successful businessperson winning, remember that everything is transactional. In life, you get out what you put in, and at some point in time, a transaction has taken place. Somewhere down the line, that athlete or businessperson paid the price to achieve their goal. The reality is that there are no shortcuts or discounts. The price to pay is usually hard work.

And while we are here, let's delve into the hard work a bit more. This can oftentimes be subjective, depending on who you talk to. If you were to ask me during my rookie season in the NFL, "Larry were you a hard worker?" my answer would have unequivocally been yes. I was never late for a meeting, and I did exactly what the coaches asked me to do. I did what every other player was asked to do. When I finished doing what the coaches required, I went home and played *Call of Duty* and *Madden* to decompress. My NFL workday was from seven o'clock in the morning until about five thirty in the afternoon.

When I arrived in Jacksonville, the organization had just signed a three-time Pro Bowler from the Green Bay Packers. Over the course of my rookie year, I noticed that the Pro Bowler always seemed to be doing extra work! I would often catch him in the training room working with the trainers, or in the cold tub getting the soreness out of his legs. I remember walking into the meeting room one morning to catch some extra z's before the day got started. He was watching extra film.

I started to see that there are levels to hard work. There are some individuals who will work really hard but only do what is required. There are some who will work hard, but every now and then they'll skip some reps when they get a little tired. Then you have the players who will do what is required and more. They will watch extra film, lift extra weights, eat nutritiously, and get plenty of sleep at night. They will also sacrifice time with their friends to put in extra work.

In reality, football is a sacrifice. Let's be clear: sacrifice is defined as giving up something of value for something regarded as more important or worthy. It is difficult at times to sacrifice what you want to do with friends or family to help better yourself on the field. Let me also mention that there is still room to enjoy yourself and have a good time, while also bettering yourself. The main thing is that you begin to understand what it is really going to take to get where you want to be.

Since sacrifice is inevitable in this game, it is very important to know your "why." Why do you want to play college football? It is critical to understand your "why" because at some point, you will be challenged. Human nature does not want to get out of its comfort zone. If you want to be an athlete at the collegiate level, your comfort zone will be challenged. Having the ability to go back to your "why" will be imperative to fall back on during the challenging times.

Let's say all of your friends are going out to a local fast-food hotspot to eat and post up after practice, and they invite you to go. The girl from math class who you have a crush on is going too. Now, you know that you are trying to lose ten pounds to improve your body composition and become quicker on the field. Or let's say all of your friends are going home right after practice to play franchise on *Madden*, but you know you need to hit the weight room to get a little stronger. What will you do?

Your goals and what you are trying to achieve will meet a challenge. The choice is obviously yours, and the question is: what will you do? The decisions we make will ultimately define who we are. I love this quote by Aristotle:

> **"WE ARE WHAT WE REPEATEDLY DO. EXCELLENCE, THEN, IS NOT AN ACT, BUT A HABIT."**

Habits will naturally set in on us. With that in mind, what habits are you building? Knowing your "why" is the foundation that will allow you to break bad habits or continue to build good ones.

The truth is you can somewhat fake it in high school, where
your talent and peer pressure can carry you, but *you've gotta
love the game* to be successful at the next level of play. How do
Thanksgiving and Christmas holidays spent away from home and
with your football family sound? You're looking at a commitment
of six to seven days per week in-season. When true passion for
the game is lacking, I have seen players walk away from full-ride
scholarships. No, I'm not kidding. I have literally seen players give
up playing football to just go to school full-time.

Without knowing your "why," you may find yourself in a deeply
unmotivated state when things become difficult or challenging
(and it is not a matter of if, it's *when*). As a result, you will be
unproductive. I remember a couple of instances when players came
up against adversity. Two of them failed out of school, and another
just gave up football. When you have that solid foundation and keep
your vision at the forefront, you will always be able to bounce back.
For example, when you know that you are pursuing a professional
career in football for your family, and/or your future family when
you are a husband and father in the coming years, it keeps things
in perspective.

You will be able to continue to get up early in the morning for those
six o'clock workouts. You keep pushing in the classroom. Keeping
your "why" in perspective will help you maintain a positive attitude
toward coaches and teammates. Yes, there will be times when
you don't feel like having a good attitude or going to class. What
separates players who are successful from those who are not is the
ability to choose to do the right things regardless of how they feel.
It really all lies in successful players' ability to consistently do more
than what is required. The behavior they demonstrate is a lifestyle.
Simply put, it is who they are.

One of the most talked about topics in recruiting among college football coaches is trying to figure out whether or not a recruit really loves the game. College football is a step up from high school and is extremely competitive. Every player on those teams was usually one of the best on their high school team. Physically, you will lift and run more than you did in high school. Mentally, the playbook will be more challenging to learn. And emotionally, you will be challenged in different areas because (many times) you will be distanced from home and family.

NEED HELP FRAMING YOUR "WHY" OR ADDING PERSPECTIVE TO HOW THE DECISIONS YOU ARE MAKING TIE INTO YOUR SUCCESS? HERE IS A SERIES OF QUESTIONS THAT ALL RECRUITS SHOULD ASK THEMSELVES AND ANSWER HONESTLY:

1. What are your goals in life? (List at least three goals.) Consider what goes into goal setting. Why are goals important?
2. How long have you been playing football? What are your football goals?
3. The choices you make are important. Think of a choice you made recently and describe how the choice impacted you at the time and will impact you in the future.
4. Consider how the choices you make impact your ability to achieve your football goals.
5. Explain the steps you plan to take to achieve each of your life and football goals.

EXTENSION ACTIVITY: VISION BOARDS

The Task: Vision boards are collages of images and words cut from magazines that describe an individual's goals for the future (such as career, hobbies, where they hope to live, etc.). Take a piece of posterboard, glue, scissors, and a stack of magazines. Flip through the magazines to find images and words that describe your goals for the future. Cut out the items representing your goals and paste those items on your posterboard, creating a collage.

Supplies: magazines, posterboard, glue, and scissors.

Extension: Have students present and share the vision boards to their classmates and/or teammates.

HERE IS AN EXAMPLE OF A DAILY SCHEDULE FOR STUDENT-ATHLETES:

- 7:00 to 8:00 a.m.: Academic meetings (Mondays only).
- 8:00 a.m. to 2:00 p.m.: Classes are held between these times.
- 2:15 p.m.: Special teams meeting.
- 2:30 to 3:15 p.m.: Position meetings.
- 3:30 to 5:30 p.m.: Practice.
- 6:30 to 7:30 p.m.: Study hall.

Obviously, game day is on Saturday and most teams have some sort of practice on Sundays.

Football translates very closely to life. It's a team sport and no one wins a championship alone. You are going to need coaches, trainers, equipment, operations, and teammates, all working together to achieve the common goal. Likewise, your goal is to put yourself in a position to play college football. Therefore, you will need a team to help you get there. You need coaches, parents/family, guidance counselors, teachers, principals, and support staff. That's your team! Remember that your team plays a vital role on your journey to becoming the student-athlete you need to be. I came across this quote a couple of years ago and it resonated with me because it applied to my life heavily:

> **"IF YOU WANT TO GO FAST, GO ALONE. IF YOU WANT TO GO FAR, GO TOGETHER."**

(I'm a freaking football coach; forgive me for all the motivational quotes! Quotes and sayings are a rite of passage in coaching; every coach has them.)

I was very close to deciding to go to the Army out of high school. I was frustrated with my poor choices, the lack of scholarship offers, and the few recruitment opportunities I had coming out of high school. However, I truly believed deep down that I was a really good football player. On that point, I am very thankful for my eldest brother, Ken. I went to him and told him my plans to join the Army, because the only opportunity I had was a 50 percent offer to play for Holmes Community College. I think he could tell deep down how badly I still wanted to play football. He encouraged me to not give up on it. He advised me to take the only offer I had, make good on it, and keep pursuing my dream. As I did then, and to this very day,

I often look to Ken for wise counsel and direction. I am so glad he steered me in that direction of my destiny, as it has truly paid off.

HERE IS A GOOD STOPPING POINT TO DO AN EXERCISE. ASK YOURSELF:

1. What is perseverance?
2. Why is perseverance an important attribute to have?
3. What area of your life could perseverance be applied to?
4. Do your opportunities have to be perfectly packaged in order for you to notice and accept them?

This is just one of the many stories where I can personally pinpoint how others have greatly impacted my life. Likewise, every student-athlete will need others to help them achieve their goal. It could be a coach, counselor, parent, sibling, or a teammate. It is extremely important to appreciate the value of having good people around you who can speak into your life. Having positive influences will help you get to the next level. There could be a time where you need encouragement, advice, or somebody to hold you accountable. All of these things play a vital role in you becoming the best person and student-athlete possible.

These relationships will also help you find your "why" and set a solid foundation for yourself as a student-athlete moving forward. For example, my high school head coach taught me toughness and respect. A big lesson I learned from my parents was to be a genuine and kind person. My older brother taught me to think bigger and go for my dreams. My wife, Juliet, imparted the importance of having supreme self-confidence and sharpness. If you pay attention as a student-athlete, there are lessons to be learned from the people around you. There are also lessons to be learned from the people around you who are making the mistakes. Stay woke.

During difficult times, where do you stand? When your body is hurting and you're not feeling your best, how do you respond? What would the teacher in your least favorite subject say about your work ethic and attitude? I enjoy asking my recruits that question to hear their *(sometimes awkward)* responses. The truth behind the answer gives me a small glimpse into a player's effort level when things are not necessarily at their preferred level of comfort. This is important.

Here is a side note that recruits should understand: College coaches evaluate everything you say and do when they communicate with you. Be yourself, but also treat every interaction as if you were interviewing for a job.

One example comes to mind from the recruiting trail where I offered a player a full, committable scholarship. He was a junior college (JUCO) player and could enroll in school mid-term, which is highly attractive to college coaches. As a mid-term enrollee, the player can enroll in school for the spring semester. When I offered the kid a scholarship, it was his only offer at the time.

In keeping with proper protocol, I decided to get the recruit on the phone with the head coach. A phone call with the head coach is usually a significant sign that school is very interested. During the call (and only during the call), this particular recruit went on to say that he was uncertain about the decision to enroll early. The reason behind it was because he wanted to play the waiting game and potentially enroll at (or wait for an offer from) a larger school. Now, this is not the end all be all, but when you say this to a coach, that tells them something about you and the value you place on the opportunities you have been afforded. This is especially true if you only have one offer and you've been sitting in JUCO for two years.

As coaches, we were hoping to hear a guy who was fired up to have a full scholarship and play Division I FBS football. Instead, we got the feeling of lukewarmth, which is not good. We were really polite with the recruit, told him to keep working hard, and wished him the very best. Immediately after that phone call, the head coach and I knew in our minds we were about to move on to another prospect and not invest as much into that recruit.

Right, wrong, or indifferent, I thought to myself, "If this guy can't appreciate the opportunity he has in front of him, how will he appreciate being here?" If he doesn't understand that we are currently his *only* offer, and he is not excited, then something is a little off. I questioned his desire to really play football. To be clear, this may or may not be the case, but it certainly is the perception. And the perception cost him an offer. This recruit could have been the greatest, most motivated student-athlete ever, but those are the thoughts that were crossing our minds on the call. Again, treat everything and every opportunity with value, as thousands of dollars are potentially being invested. Treat it as you would an interview and a valuable opportunity.

Similar to life, in football, one will need a game plan or strategy to execute. As coaches, we go into every game doing our best to think of every possible scenario that may occur and have a plan of attack for it. As a student-athlete, you will need to have a game plan for your life. At this stage, that plan entails knowing NCAA and graduation requirements, knowing the benefits of becoming an early enrollee and deciding if it would work for you, and building your brand. There is much to unpack here.

So I'll ask again—is football what *you* really want? If the answer is an emphatic "YES!"—awesome, that leads us to the steps of building your game plan. We'll discuss the key, foundational points that will give you a leg up on and off the field.

CONVERSATION STARTERS:

1. What's your relationship with football? Would you consider it "love"?
2. What's your "why" and source of motivation?
3. What are your long-term goals for football?
4. Do you consider football a sacrifice? Why or why not?
5. Do you plan on playing in the NFL?
6. Why do you want to play college football?
7. What is your response when something frustrates you?
8. What will motivate you to push when you're tired or sore?
9. Can you describe your game plan or strategy to pursue your football dreams?
10. What does it mean to treat every recruiting opportunity as if it were an interview?
11. What are the biggest positives and challenges of being a student-athlete, in your opinion?
12. In the foreword, Rashad Jennings mentions the "noise" and "voices in the recruitment process (and the game of football in general) that can either lift you up or tear you down." What do you think that means?

HUDDLE UP: SECTION REVIEW

☐   What key takeaways and new information have you learned?

_____

_____

_____

_____

☐   How has this new information changed your thinking about
    your current commitment to playing football at the next level
    and your next steps in the recruitment process?

_____

_____

_____

_____

☐   Are there any adjustments that need to be made?

_____

_____

_____

_____

CHAPTER 2
SEPARATE YOURSELF (O)

Steve Campbell, former head football coach at the University of South Alabama, always talks about the world being "full of average." In his raspy Southern accent, Campbell encourages players to "be somebody special." It takes doing more than what's required.

Typically, every Division I football program will have approximately 120 players on their roster. There are eleven starters on offense and eleven starters on defense. When we factor in the back-ups, that brings the total up to forty-four players. Usually, these forty-four players are the ones primarily playing in games. That means that around 60 percent of the team will not play in the game.

I remember at one of my coaching jobs, we had an opening once. We posted on Football Scoop that we were looking for applicants. Football Scoop is a very popular media outlet among coaches. It is a website that posts new hires and openings across college and professional football. Needless to say, we received well over one hundred résumés for the position. The number of inquiries we had about the position was unbelievable. To take it a step further, it was an entry-level position with low pay. Standing out among the masses was key to landing the job, and the same goes for recruiting prospects.

According to the NCAA, as a recruit, you need to separate yourself from a little over one million other athletes playing high school football. Everyone in your high school will take classes, lift weights, and practice with the team. Hypothetically, if there was a job opening at a college that was only accepting résumés from recruits, and thousands of résumés were submitted, where would you rank among the masses? Would your résumé stand out among those that were sent? How would you separate yourself from the pack?

As mentioned earlier, to separate yourself, would you be willing to:

- Spend an extra thirty minutes after practice perfecting your craft daily?
- Sacrifice an after-school nap to watch some extra film?
- Go to the weight room to get an extra lift?
- Sacrifice playing *Call of Duty* with the guys to study for the next morning's exam?

Watching film is a great way to separate yourself and hone your craft. Film watching can be done effectively in many different ways.

TRY THIS:

Visit your coach during their office hours and ask them to watch some practice film with you. Tell them to go into detail about some things you could improve upon. Another way is to simply pull up YouTube and search coaching drills. Yes, I admit I have done this myself as a player and as a coach, and there are some great things to be found. You will find that some big names in coaching have shared a lot of their drills, or there could be coaches just talking through football. This will increase your overall football IQ. There are also plenty of clinic films available on YouTube for your viewing pleasure. This information can help you better understand the nuances of football, which will help you better prepare to excel in the game.

I recall instances while playing in the NFL when my position coach would show us how to pull up certain cut-ups. Cut-ups are basically specific clips of film that have been grouped together as a tool for player development. For example, coach would find all of the sacks a specific player made in the last two seasons and group them together for us to watch consecutively. He watched film with us during position meetings with our group to address challenges and took the time to explain and show us how to use the software to find meaningful cut-ups to best hone our craft. Most coaches access their film through Hudl. Hudl is a software program most high schools use to record practice and games. Players can access their film via Hudl and can choose particular plays during a game to make up their highlight tape to share on social media for recruiting coaches to view.

I highly recommend asking your coach about cut-ups or film for your specific position, as well as how to use Hudl.

Let's say ten hours per week is what your coach requires from every player on your team. Are you willing to put in five or more hours on top of what's required? As a football coach, it is very clear who puts in extra work. Hear me out: I am not at all against having a good time, but as my dad always told me, "Business before pleasure, son." Who is willing to make changes to their daily routine to put themselves ahead of their competitors?

Coaches often use this phrase, "He's just a football player." This phrase encompasses a couple different things. It means that the player naturally has a knack for doing things well on the field. Coaches do not have to explain things to him, he just does it naturally and usually at a high level. It also refers to an individual who loves the game. Simply put, football is innate and would appear to be in the player's blood, part of his DNA. He loves everything about the sport: the weightlifting, the competition, grueling practices, and all the wonderful things football has to offer.

Separate yourself as an athlete and recruit by developing the habits of being on time, being unselfish, working hard, being competitive, having a good attitude, and bringing positive energy. These attributes should embody who you are on and off the field. How you do anything is how you do everything. If you decide that you want to become a college football player, then allow yourself to have those positive qualities that stand out to coaches and teammates. With practice and effort, working hard, showing up with a good attitude, and bringing positive energy day in, day out, can become second nature.

Work on being so great that if, by chance, you show up late to a meeting or have a bad attitude, then all of the coaches will be completely shocked and caught off guard, as they are used to you being consistent and carrying yourself as a professional. Let's keep this in perspective: I'm not saying that football should control your entire life. However, I am saying that if something is really important to you, then there are certain attributes that come along with that. This is how you separate yourself.

What I have found is that there are a lot of players who love the *idea* of football versus actually loving football and everything that it entails. They love the idea of having a full scholarship and fans cheering. They love the idea of having people around campus looking at them in admiration, and that is what is most desirable in their minds. However, loving everything that football includes, even the difficult things, is the attribute recruits should desire to have. As a coach, this is the type of player everyone wants to have in their program. This is also a quality any employer would want to have on their team. If all other things are equal, and you display this quality, who do you think will get ahead or separate themselves?

I remember one spring, I was very fortunate to have a lot of depth at one of the positions I was coaching. I had three players who were really good athletes. All of them had good size, speed, and strength. They all had the physical qualities to be really good players. I knew the competition to win the starting job would be challenging. Separating yourself is no easy task. As the saying goes:

"THERE ARE NO TRAFFIC JAMS ALONG THE EXTRA MILE."
—ROGER STAUBACH

The battle for the starting position continued all the way through the end of fall camp. It was a difficult decision, but I settled on a starter. Shortly after playing a couple of games that season, I noticed that the backup actually shined more in games than the starter did. Around game three, I made a switch, and the backup became the starter. There was something else I continued to notice: the backup was always on time, always had a positive attitude, and I always caught him in the weight room doing additional time. Even as a backup, he was willing to put in extra work, and that work eventually allowed him to shine and surpass his competition.

When you are consistent in your approach every day, the results you're looking for will eventually come. This guy didn't complain or become a negative teammate; he just kept showing up and working hard. He put in extra work, and he always knew what to do when his number was called. When he got his opportunity, he shined. These actions ultimately led to him becoming the starter by the third week of the season. It didn't happen immediately or as fast as he wanted it to, but he kept pushing. Likewise, it is important for you to keep pushing and doing things the correct way, even when it gets tough.

Your decisions are important, especially those decisions that will affect the outcome of your life. Therefore, don't leave anything up to chance. Control what you can control. I can't control my genetics or what colleges decide to offer me. However, I can control things such as my academics, my attitude, my work ethic, how I treat people, and being the best version of myself that I can be. There is a 50/50 shot that leaving things up to chance could work out in your favor. However, there is much stronger evidence of the negative outcomes associated with failure to plan, failure to act on the necessary things in life, and taking an overall lackadaisical approach to your future.

Are you lax as a high school prospect?

LET'S CHECK:

☐ Have you met with your guidance counselor to check on your schedule and compare it to your school's 48H form? (We will discuss the 48H in more detail later.)

☐ Do you have an after-practice regimen? What does it entail?

☐ How much time do you devote to extra film study each week?

☐ On a scale of one to ten, how would you rate your football IQ? Could you have a conversation with a college recruiter and describe the nuances of your offensive or defensive scheme?

☐ How many coaches have you sent your Hudl film to?

Separate Yourself: The How-To

On the field: Performance matters—*a lot!*

What you put on the field for coaches to see matters. Be dominant on your high school team. Are you:

- ☐ Showing up on the field and standing out?
- ☐ Putting up numbers and great stats?
- ☐ Making big plays?

These attributes will lead to good Hudl film, which is vital.

Here is a Hudl tip: arrange your best and most explosive clips first. College coaches watch hours and hours of recruiting film. You need to catch their eye immediately and arrange your film with the goal of *keeping* their attention. Continue to add newer, more explosive clips and keep your Hudl film fresh. There are some players out there that coaches really like and they want to keep evaluating. So anytime you have more Hudl film to add, keep updating it as much as possible.

When viewing film, college coaches are mainly looking for:

→ **SHOWCASE OF SPEED**

This is where the player can show either going for a touchdown or running across the field to make a tackle. The coaches want to see the player sprint at top speed on film.

→ PHYSICAL PLAY

This can be an offensive lineman pulling or knocking over a defender, a running back, or wide receiver running somebody over. It could be a defender who comes in for a tackle very aggressively. Coaches are looking for extremely aggressive players.

→ ABILITY TO CHANGE DIRECTION

We like to see a player sprinting at full speed in one direction and suddenly stop and go in another direction. This will show the coaching staff hip mobility and see if you show signs of stiffness or not.

→ EXPLOSIVENESS AND TWITCH

Think of this as acceleration: how fast can you get your momentum going? This can be a running back making a cut and accelerating through the hole, or a defender quickly exploding into a blocker.

One of things coaches love to see are kids who show a lot of effort. I remember my special teams coach in the NFL giving a speech to the team and he said, "Effort over time equals success." This equation can apply to any situation and has stuck with me. I apply it to a lot of areas of my life, and I encourage you to do the same. When you are on the football field, make it a point to outwork your opponent. Play harder and longer than the person you are going against. Apply this to any situation; work harder and longer than anyone else. I can assure you if you do this consistently and make this a priority in your life, success is sure to find you. Make sure this mindset and ideal shows up on your Hudl film, and in as many areas of your life as possible.

Off the field: Become a *professional*.

These are necessary considerations in addition to your required activities with your team.

➜   **BE COACHABLE.**

First and foremost, be coachable. As a player, you should want coaches to be on you about your academics and challenge you in any and all areas that need improvement. You should want coaches to push you to be the best version of yourself on and off the field. Accountability doesn't always feel great, but it's extremely important to personal development. I have come across many players, and people in general, who get defensive when held accountable for their actions. Instead, try embracing it and watch your level of growth skyrocket. Word to the wise: welcome accountability with open arms.

I have seen it as a player and while I have been coaching. A guy can have a lot of ability and could be a really good football player, but he may struggle with being coachable. He struggles to listen, or he hates when someone is getting on his case about something. On multiple occasions, I have seen kids transfer or be ineffective due to being uncoachable.

➜   **LEARN TRUE RESPONSIBILITY.**

Right now, if you are a teen growing into adulthood and making key decisions for your life, it is time to take responsibility. This lesson is crucial, and the sooner we delve into how to do this effectively, the better. I highly encourage each young person I interact with to take ownership of themselves. Start learning how to self-advocate and problem solve. If you're struggling in a class, go speak with your teacher one-on-one and ask for help. Don't wait for your parents to initiate contact or for poor grades and test scores to be posted before you take action. Take the initiative. Start asking questions and set plans in motion that will benefit you.

As soon as I got into coaching, I remember hearing players complain randomly about the cafeteria food not being good. The coaches would give the old boring speech about being appreciative of their free meal, and the players would oftentimes roll their eyes and go on to talk about how the cafe needs to be better. "How can you expect us to go out there and give it our all on the field if we don't have proper nutrition?" they would say.

First, there were always nutritious meals in the cafe, they just didn't like their options, or how they were prepared, or whatever else they could complain about. There was always fruit, bagels, hot meals, salads, and all kinds of other options. Secondly, it never ever fails that when a player graduates from college and the free meals stop, they always come back around to say how much they miss the cafe.

Why the change of heart all of a sudden? The players now understand and appreciate true responsibility. When they learned about the costs of living in the real world and saw how they added up, they began to appreciate what they used to have for free. The costs of food, apartment, car insurance, cell phone, and other expenses were now all on them, and it did not sit well. As the old adage goes,

> **"YOU NEVER MISS YOUR WATER UNTIL YOUR WELL RUNS DRY."**

It is extremely important for a young person to learn to take
responsibility for their life. Learn the critical lesson of how to ask
questions and take initiative. Don't sit around and wait on people
to do things for you. When you graduate from college and you're
out there in the world on your own, if people do things for you, that
does not help your development. So start learning these critical
skills now. This will help you become a better football player
and person.

During the 2019 season, the Baltimore Ravens shared the slogan,
"No one cares, work harder." Although quite a blunt way to put it,
this phrase holds major truth. Everyone has a story, everyone has
issues, but excuses and blame won't get you where you want to go.
Save it and put that energy into doing the work. I tell players all the
time that if they don't take care of themselves, who will? If you don't
learn to be proactive and work hard for yourself, who will? I'm not
saying there aren't people in the position to lend a helping hand,
but I'm encouraging you to see the help as an added bonus, not as
an expectation.

Life will throw unforeseen circumstances your way. I'm
encouraging you to develop the mindset of a problem solver. It's
hard to beat the guy who never quits. Sometimes, life will present
challenges that are not your fault, such as troubled home life,
injuries, disappointments, and meager finances. Find a way to keep
pushing forward and avoid the "blame game." Learn to use your
stumbling blocks as stepping-stones. While I was growing up, my
dad would encourage me to "keep a smile on my face and a smile in
my heart." As difficult as that may be, I'd like to encourage you in
the same manner. *Practice makes perfect!*

→   HONE YOUR CRAFT.

Here are some examples of position-specific drills to practice:

1. **Receivers:** Catch ball(s), run routes, ball security
2. **Tight Ends:** Blocking, run routes, ball security
3. **Defensive Backs:** Footwork, man technique, zone drops
4. **Offensive Line:** Pass-and-run block technique
5. **Defensive Line:** Block destruct technique, pass rush
6. **Running Backs:** Ball security, footwork, vision
7. **Linebackers:** Tackling, footwork, zone drops
8. **Quarterbacks:** Throwing, footwork, ball security

Get with coaches to find more specific drills that will allow you to get better at your position. Do some research and use YouTube as a free resource as well. For example: Brent Venables, defensive coordinator at Clemson University, is regarded as one of the best defensive minds in all of college football. He has posted a teaching tape for the linebacker position on YouTube for use and has slides on the video giving descriptions and coaching points for his players. Go to YouTube.com and type in Brent Venables LB drills.

Karl Scott, who is currently the defensive backs coach for the Minnesota Vikings, also has a video on YouTube for free public use describing coverages he ran while he was at the University of Alabama.

These videos posted by football greats are available on YouTube, and this valuable, free knowledge can help you grow your skillset as an aspiring college athlete. As a coach, I am constantly trying to stretch myself mentally, and as a player, so should you. This is yet another aspect that separates the "greats" from the pack. Any player can look up information for their specific positions on YouTube or via a quick Google search. Thanks to the World Wide Web, there are amazing materials available to you, free of charge.

SNAPSHOT:

If you are a receiver, you should catch balls after practice. Also, train to become more durable by working on your core, hamstrings, and smaller muscles. These are the little things that athletes often overlook.

➔ **TAKE CARE OF YOUR BODY.**

From my personal playing experience to now observing as a coach, I've noticed that most athletic injuries occur at your **joints and hinges**: ankles, knees, wrists, shoulders, hips, etc. I stumbled across an article from the University of Pittsburgh Medical Center that confirms this and a few more common injuries among athletes.

Specifically for football players, weight training and conditioning are extremely important. At the forefront of your mind should be injury prevention. Getting your muscles bigger will allow you the ability to take on the physical impact that the sport of football inevitably demands. Conditioning allows you to maintain proper posture in practice and in games. You can be as big and strong as you want; however, if you are not conditioned, it will not work out well. You will need stamina to be able to last multiple plays in a row.

Many high school athletes focus on lifting weights as the main aspect of their conditioning. And while that is important, be sure to also spend ample time stretching and training the smaller muscle groups to help prevent injury. Flexibility (and increasing your range of motion) is key to injury prevention. Ever tried yoga or Pilates? According to articles from *Men's Journal* and CNBC, Aaron Rodgers and Odell Beckham Jr. are two notable NFL players who practice yoga. When I played in the NFL and during the regular season, we were provided free weekly yoga classes. It helps! When I played professionally, core strength was an issue for me. So yoga poses helped me with my core strength, stretching, and strengthening smaller muscles. If you are unfamiliar with yoga, give it a try. While the benefits of yoga are great, if you're not interested in becoming a "yogi," there are more options out there to achieve measurable results. Speak with your athletic trainer or coach about helpful exercises to aid in building core strength, stretching techniques, and increased flexibility.

Taking care of your body will help you excel on the field. If you are in tip top shape, that will help your chances of getting playing time, as well as increase your ability to make plays when the opportunity presents itself. It is common to see college football players have issues with their weight, especially during fall camp and spring training. I have seen players lose ten to fifteen pounds over a two-week span, and with it, their strength and power declines as well. Or, on the other end of the spectrum, some guys will be overweight and will need to spend valuable training time getting back in shape. These issues are detrimental to the business plan. It's extremely important to maintain your weight and strength. Failure to do so will have an impact on your productivity and could hurt your chances of getting on the field. Therefore, think of your body as something that needs constant maintenance and care. It needs your attention every day (i.e., cold tub, hot tub, stretching, weights).

Ask the athletic trainers at your school to show you how to best take care of your body. Have them give you different exercises to strengthen the muscles around your joints and hinges. For example: ask for specific exercises and stretches to help prevent hamstring pulls. I mention this in particular, as hamstring pulls are extremely common among football athletes. Usually, these types of pulls plague skill players the most, since they do a lot of running and changing direction during practice and games, making them the most susceptible. Groin issues are extremely frequent as well.

I know it's cliché, but the following three aspects of your health (especially when it comes to your body's overall performance) are essential:

CHECKUP:

Are you:
☐ Getting enough sleep (eight hours)?
☐ Eating as best you can? (I know it's hard!)
☐ Drinking plenty of water?

Tip: According to US News Health, divide your body weight in half and try to drink that amount in ounces each day. When practicing or playing, add to your standard daily ounces.

When you don't get enough water, every cell of your body is affected. According to US News Health, when you sweat, you lose electrolytes, including sodium, potassium, and chloride, which are essential to your body's functions. Pretty much all of your cellular communications revolve around sodium and potassium, including muscle contractions and action potentials. This is why you will often cramp when you work out without proper hydration.

Back in my high school days, it was common for athletes to walk around school with gallon jugs of water to finish throughout the day. Is that still a thing?

➜   **SHARPEN YOUR FOOTBALL IQ.**

Learn and be able to explain football fundamentals as they relate to your specific position group. When you show up to football camps and "talk football" with recruiting coaches, it is an added bonus if you are knowledgeable. Start having conversations with your coach to sharpen your football IQ. For example: ask your coach to explain the route tree, cover three versus quarters coverages, 3rd down versus 4th down fronts, etc. If you can communicate and show solid football knowledge with your coach, you can do so with a recruiter as well.

Practice this. Here are more examples of position-specific football skills to know:

1. **Receivers & Defensive Backs:** Route tree and coverages
2. **Offensive Line:** Fronts and protections
3. **Defensive Line:** Gaps and techniques
4. **Running Backs:** Blitz pickup
5. **Tight Ends:** Route tree and blocking technique
6. **Linebackers:** Coverages and fits
7. **Quarterbacks:** Weakness in coverages to aid in decision-making

→ **DON'T BE A "ONE-TRICK PONY."**

It's so important for student-athletes to be *well-rounded*. Doing so gives you the ability to relate to more people, which in itself is worthwhile, as the ability to network and make connections is very important in life. Work to broaden your knowledge so that you can relate to more people, practice time management skills, and better yourself as a person in the process.

Correspondingly, you're at the beginning stages of being intentional about developing the professional skills that you will need in life. Without spreading yourself too thin, be selective and choose to be involved in the things that truly allow your passions to shine through. High school athletes should start sharpening their skills and showing their versatility by expanding their brand and taking action steps, such as joining clubs and organizations, engaging in community service and volunteer work, being a multi-sport athlete, and serving in a youth leadership capacity at school and/or in the community. Add these details to your résumé. College coaches are definitely big on players who play multiple sports, as that speaks to their athleticism and their ability to multitask. Colleges are looking to build a diverse student body and include significant questions and essay prompts on college applications. Be prepared to shine in your best light and showcase yourself!

BRAINSTORMING ACTIVITY: ARE YOU CHECKING ALL OF THE BOXES AS A HIGH SCHOOL ATHLETE AND COLLEGE-BOUND PROSPECT?

☐ GPA and test scores meet the NCAA sliding scale requirements
☐ Multi-sport athlete

- **Pro Tip:** Track & field is highly favorable to college coaches, as it teaches proper running form and can help to build and showcase speed. Recruiting coaches often attend track meets.
- ☐ Participation in clubs and organizations
- ☐ Brand-building on Twitter (clean your social media footprint)
- ☐ Volunteer work and service hours

CONVERSATION STARTERS:

1. Football translates to life very closely. It's a team sport—no one wins a championship alone. From family members to school staff to coaches, who are your team members? List the names of the people you consider to be a part of your *team* to help you succeed.

2. What would the teacher in your least favorite subject say about your work ethic and attitude?

3. In this chapter, I mention the world being "full of average," and how head coach Steve Campbell encourages players to "be somebody special." What does that mean to you? Can you apply that to your life experiences thus far? How can this idea be applied to your future?

4. Pick three of the quotes below from *The Recruit's Playbook* (or all of them!), and in three to four sentences, explain their meanings in your own words:
   - "There are no traffic jams along the extra mile."
   - "Work beats talent, when talent doesn't work hard."
   - "No one cares, work harder."

- "...there's no comparison between the sun and the moon. They shine when it's their time."
- "Comparison is the thief of joy."

5. What main things are coaches looking for in your Hudl film?

6. What does it mean to "be coachable"? Why is this important on and off the field?

7. In this chapter, I advise players to avoid being a "one-trick pony." Research the origin of this idiom and explain its figurative and literal meaning. What advice am I giving players with the use of this idiom?

8. I advise players to talk with their coaches about specific drills that will allow them to become better at their position and enhance their football IQ. What are some position-specific drills that will help you and why? Jot those down.

9. Fill-in-the-Blank: Most athletic injuries occur at your _____: ankles, knees, wrists, shoulders, hips, etc. Why do you think that's the case? What should you do to help prevent injury?

10. How much water should you drink in a day? (*Hint*: there's a math problem in *The Recruit's Playbook*.) How do you calculate the number of ounces?

HUDDLE UP: SECTION REVIEW

☐ What key takeaways and new information have you learned in this chapter about how to separate yourself as an aspiring college athlete and hone your craft?

_____

_____

_____

_____

☐ How has what you learned changed your plan for standing out among your fellow athletes?

_____

_____

_____

_____

☐ **Self-Assessment:** What does your level of play on your Hudl film say to recruiting coaches—fair, average, above average, or "shark in a fish tank"? Honest answers only.

_____

_____

_____

_____

CHAPTER 3

ONE SIZE DOES NOT FIT ALL (X)

As the saying goes, "...there's no comparison between the sun and the moon. They shine when it's their time." Getting a firm grasp on this idea and avoiding comparison is key for recruitment, as well as for life.

The recruiting process looks different for each individual player and will vary based on genetics, physical development, academics, and injury, among other things. Factors beyond our control such as height and body frame play a crucial role in how the recruitment journey will unfold for each student-athlete.

Some may start being recruited and receiving offers in their freshman year of high school, and others may not start getting attention or receiving offers until their senior season. Or like me, some may have no interest or offers and attend junior college on a half scholarship, *and that's okay.* Initially, my recruitment was extremely slow due to my height (I was five feet eleven inches in high school) and poor academics. Some guys simply need more time to develop in order to reach their full potential.

Let's say you are a great athlete, but you're undersized for your position. You can be recruited, earn a scholarship, and be successful playing at the next level. Be aware that a recruiting coach may be looking for you to have other exceptional talents to make up for being undersized. For example, if you're an undersized quarterback (QB), you typically have to possess great speed and arm strength to balance out your size. If your speed and arm talent are similar to a player who is taller, a Division I school will most likely extend an offer to the prospect who has better size. But don't be discouraged, keep getting better. Favorable height and weight, as well as what is considered undersized, varies by position. A great example of this is Tyreek Hill of the Kansas City Chiefs. He stands at a mere five feet nine inches, but he makes up for his size with freakishly elite speed (as evidenced by a forty-yard dash time of 4.29 seconds).

As mentioned above, I was five feet, eleven inches coming out of high school. I was considered undersized for the defensive end position. Thankfully, I possessed some qualities that helped make up for my lack of size. For example, my quickness and speed gave me an advantage over taller individuals. I was able to develop this agility through powerlifting. Olympic lifts, tire pulls, and running regime also played a huge role in my athletic maturation process.

There are many young athletes who utilize track and field as a means to develop speed and quickness. I tried track and field, but after almost breaking something trying to jump over hurdles, I quickly realized that I was better off going a different route before injuring myself and thus defeating the entire point. Also, once I added up all of the extra training and conditioning that track and field would require, I gracefully bowed out and decided that the best option for me was to stick to powerlifting. Find what fits you best and get after it. An article in *USA Today* stated that twenty-two of thirty-two first picks in the NFL draft participated in track and field in high school, so there's definitely something to it. Only three players out of thirty-two first round picks were not multi-sport athletes in high school.

It is important to understand that your path may look different from others. I had to go the junior college route, but some players go straight to larger universities right out of high school. The point I am making—one I do my best to instill in the guys I coach—is to run your race and focus on becoming the best version of yourself. Never ever lose confidence, and keep your head up like your nose is bleeding.

Position	Average Height	Average Weight
Quarterback	6'3"	224.97 lbs.
Running Back	5'11"	214.48 lbs.
Wide Receiver	6'0"	200.32 lbs.
Tight End	6'4"	254.26 lbs.
Fullback	6'0"	244.43 lbs.
Offensive Line	6'4"	314.16 lbs.
Defensive Back	5'11"	200.10 lbs.
Linebacker	6'2"	244.64 lbs.
Defensive End	6'3"	278.99 lbs.
Defensive Tackle	6'3"	308.97 lbs.
Kicker	6'0"	202.58 lbs.
Punter	6'1"	214.32 lbs.
Long Snapper	6'2"	243.76 lbs.

Based on NFL Combine statistics, offensive linemen and tight ends are the tallest players on average, and running backs are the shortest players on average. Wide receivers seem to have the largest range of height of all positions. So when coaches use the term undersized, they're referring to a quarterback being six feet or six feet, one inch. He would be considered smaller than average. Another example would be an offensive lineman who is six feet, one inch, who would also be considered undersized. However, if a WR is six feet, one inch, he wouldn't be considered undersized.

We have all seen plenty of those "I was overlooked and undrafted" recounts turn into major success stories in the football industry. Keep your options open, and do not neglect or overlook opportunities in lower divisions. Look it up. There are definitely former National Association of Intercollegiate Athletics (NAIA) players turned NFL pros! According to NAIA.org, some success stories include John Kitna, Aldrick Rosas, and Krishawn Hogan.

One of my favorite examples of a lower division player turned pro is Shannon Sharpe. Shannon is an NFL Hall of Famer and former NFL All-Pro who won multiple Super Bowl championships as a player. Shannon was also selected to participate in several Pro Bowls. The Pro Bowl is a postseason game that is played by the top NFL players at their position. Shannon is currently a TV personality on the popular show *Undisputed* on Fox Sports, where he and Skip Bayless debate various sports topics.

Mr. Sharpe had a tremendous NFL career. The college he attended was Savannah State University, the oldest HBCU in the state of Georgia. At that time, Savannah State was a Division II school. He was selected in the last round of the NFL draft, and most would agree that he was overlooked. Case in point that the NFL will come and find you. The key is to be dominant and stand out at any level school you attend. Be "a shark in a fish tank" or a "big fish in a small pond," as they say. Shannon was a three-time All-American at Savannah State and put up some great numbers while he was in college. This caught the attention of scouts, and he got a chance to play in the NFL. The rest is history.

I know a lot of players will find this hard to believe, but there are some real positives to playing at smaller schools. While playing at lower-level schools, players tend to get on the field sooner than they would at larger programs. There are players from Power 5 schools who have reached out to me about transferring due to a lack of playing time. The goal here is not to convince you to give on your dream of going Power 5, but rather to present another perspective as a backup idea.

At the end of the day, I encourage athletes to run their own race. They say, "comparison is the thief of joy," and I can agree with that. You cannot be at the top of your game while focusing on and comparing your recruiting situation to the guy next to you.

Your journey is just that: *your own.*

CONVERSATION STARTERS:

1. What's your relationship with football? Would you consider it "love"?
2. What's your "why" and source of motivation?
3. What are your long-term goals for football?
4. Do your height and weight align (or have the potential to align) with NFL averages, or would you be considered undersized like myself?
5. If undersized, what are some things you can do to help overcome this?
6. Imagine a scenario in which you are recruited in a different way than you had imagined. What are some things you can do to continue to mark your path toward success?

HUDDLE UP: SECTION REVIEW

☐   What key takeaways and new information have you learned
      in this chapter regarding your outlook and the path toward
      college recruitment?

      _____

      _____

      _____

      _____

CHAPTER 4
IT'S A MIND GAME (O)

Know your weaknesses. Many choose to focus on their strengths alone and, unfortunately, allow those strengths to make them feel too comfortable. In football, we often say the game is 90 percent mental and 10 percent physical. With that in mind, study what is inhibiting you from being in the best mental shape possible.

This may seem simple; however, it can be quite complex. I'm not classically trained in the art of psychology, but I know that if your state of mind is not up to par, it can cause issues, both on and off the field.

If a player finds himself about to flunk out of college and lose his scholarship due to having a low GPA, a number of factors can come into play. In the situations where kids have learning challenges, this obviously doesn't apply. But if you have full learning abilities, yet you find yourself not living up to your full potential, the question to ask yourself is: why?

If a player is consistently finding himself in trouble and making poor decisions, again, ask why. I have come across situations where kids have GPAs of around 2.7, which isn't too bad. But I know they have the ability to be at least a 3.5 student. So an important question to ask yourself is: what is holding you back from being the absolute best version of yourself?

The transition from high school to JUCO was a bit of challenge for me. It was really my first time being away from home. I am usually very quiet and reserved, so naturally it took me some time to find my niche. I struggled to maintain good grades my first semester on campus. The big thing I did in this situation was keep fighting the good fight. I went to speak to professors during their office hours, asked to redo or make up assignments for a better score, and attended extra study sessions beyond the required study hall. Eventually, it clicked for me because I refused to throw in the towel.

I encourage players to look internally as often and as deeply as possible. Study yourself. Spend time trying to understand your shortcomings and how you can improve. Do you have a poor relationship with a parent? Is there a situation that occurred when you were young that continues to weigh you down? You cannot harbor trauma for the rest of your life and still be free. It acts as a weight pulling you down to the bottom of the ocean. Are you shortchanging yourself by looking at social media, seeing how great everyone else's life appears to be and getting down on yourself?

Whatever the situation or circumstance, it is extremely important to protect your mind. In order to be the best student-athlete you can, build your mental health to prepare for the game of life. A huge factor here is that those who need help the most are usually reluctant to seek it. I know it can be quite challenging for young men to ask for help when they need it. However, it is vital to find a way to navigate through issues. What has proven most realistic is to confide in a trusted adult. In my case, my coaches and my oldest brother served as my mentors.

If problems are left alone, they will grow bigger, and more costly mistakes could be made down the road. Every year, college football players will be dismissed from their programs due to one issue or another. I am encouraging you to not allow any "foxes to continue to lie around the chicken coop," as this could prove costly and detrimental.

Everyone can benefit from some kind of wise council, whether they want to admit it or not. I encourage you to seek out your guidance counselor. Some schools even have social workers and mental health counselors on staff. You have resources, so don't be afraid to find qualified people with whom to discuss your issues. It helps. Seek professional counseling, confide in a mentor and/or trusted adult, or keep a journal. A great technique that works for me is to tap into the power of daily affirmations and positive thinking. For example, I normally tell myself on a daily basis, "I am blessed, and I will be a blessing to others. I am a great husband. I am a hard worker. I am a victor, not a victim. My future is so bright, I will need sunglasses to look at it. I am an overcomer. I have purpose." I encourage players to affirm themselves into being the type of men they want to become and claiming and manifesting the outcomes in life they wish to see.

Do not neglect your mind. Be truthful with yourself. Ask the tough questions: Am I lazy? Am I too defensive? Am I depressed? Am I hardheaded or arrogant? Am I truly okay? The list can go on and on. Don't minimize the importance of your inner work. Once you have had these real conversations with yourself, make the necessary adjustments.

Everyone's situation is different. People come from all different backgrounds. The main thing is to learn about yourself, figure out your challenges, and work to overcome them. As a coach, I have found it to be true that the kids who work to develop themselves on the inside typically improve on the field as well. Learn this lesson as early as possible.

Student-athletes are exposed to multiple stressors in addition to those of the average teenager. It is important to build your mental capacity to best handle the added pressure. Multiple factors could add stress to the lives of student-athletes: juggling classes, grades, school commitments, possibly holding down a job, and let's not underestimate the expectations of a high school coach, or being a part of a seven-on-seven team. Additionally, depending on your level of recruitment, people from recruiting websites, the media, etc. may be reaching out to get information from you.

It's not uncommon for student-athletes to take on a good amount of responsibility. These stressors can bring serious issues to the forefront. Although stress is an unavoidable aspect of the recruitment process, if unmanaged, it can prove damaging. Have discussions with your parents, build relationships with coaches, and narrow down the places you would like to attend to help alleviate the stress. Make your mental health a top priority.

According to the American Psychological Association, signs of stress in teens can show up as:
1. Irritability and anger
2. Sudden changes in behavior
3. Trouble sleeping
4. Neglecting responsibilities
5. Eating changes
6. Getting sick more often

As a coach, I notice that players who are going through stressful times display characteristics such as tardiness, mood swings, and negative overall body language. This will tell you to check on them. They also seem to have low energy or appear drained all the time. When these signs are evident, it is time to talk.

And to manage and best keep stressors at bay, the APA recommends that teens:
1. Limit screen time and sleep eight to ten hours a night.

2. Exercise. The US Department of Health and Human
    Services recommends at least sixty minutes a day of
    activity for children ages six to seventeen.
3. Talk about stressful situations with a trusted adult.
4. Make time for fun and schedule some free time.

Personally, I like to set my day as soon as I wake up. I verbalize
the type of attitude and mindset I want to have throughout the
day. Obviously, it doesn't always go as planned, but I know that it
definitely gives me the best chance of not being overwhelmed by the
daily grind. I also use exercise, video games, reading, and praying
as different ways to manage my stress. Another one of my favorite
things to do to overcome stressful situations is listen to one of my
favorite pastors deliver a message on YouTube or via podcast. I
highly recommend finding something that works for you. It is truly
important to have a positive outlet and not let things build up.

Unmanaged stress can lead to unexpected results. People react to
stress in a lot of different ways. If you're struggling to get sleep, then
you won't be able to perform to the best of your ability. If you are more
irritable and have heightened mood swings with your teammates
and/or coaches, that could produce unpleasant consequences. I get
it, trust me. As a coach, we all do. Life happens, things don't always
go as planned, and many things are outside of our control and can be
outright unfair. For that reason, stress management is important and
should not be an afterthought. It can spill over onto the football field
and turn into selfishness and a morale killer.

I had this very thing happen with a player who was having some
issues back home, and he didn't speak to anyone or handle it
properly whatsoever. Ultimately, he was suspended and his
future with the team was in jeopardy. This particular player was

also close to completing his college degree. He was allowed to return to the team, and he matured from the situation and his mistakes. However, the poor decisions he made nearly cost him the opportunity to complete his college degree for free and the opportunity to play college football. That would have been a huge price to pay for poor decision-making and mismanaged stress. Thankfully, he was given a second chance and went on to become the first person in his family to earn a college degree.

It's important to develop some form of resilience to stressful situations early on. The higher the level you go up in athletics, the more pressure there is. College football is a big-time business—the revenue college football generates nationwide is substantial. As such, athletic directors and presidents want results from their head coaches, head coaches will apply pressure to their coaches, and the coaches will apply pressure to the players. This is also consistent in professional sports—there's even more pressure added when playing in the NFL. It is important to develop good habits now, while in high school, to prepare you for what is hopefully on the horizon.

CONVERSATION STARTERS:

1. In this chapter, I mention the common idea that the game of football is 90 percent mental and 10 percent physical. What does this mean? Do you agree or disagree, and why?

2. Is there anything weighing down your mind or keeping you from being the best version of yourself? What do you do to find motivation during the tough times? Who or what inspires you or lifts your spirits?

3. What are your stressors? How do you manage stress? Are there things you can do to improve how you manage stress?

HUDDLE UP: SECTION REVIEW

☐ What key takeaways and new information have you learned
in this chapter?

_____

_____

_____

_____

☐ What are some ways that stress shows up for you? Do you
notice any effects on your body or behavior?

_____

_____

_____

_____

☐ In addition to the techniques suggested in this chapter, what
can you do to relieve stress?

_____

_____

_____

_____

KNOW THE BIZ

It's common knowledge that football is big business as well as the number one sport in the United States. With that comes over one million high school football players, of which roughly 74,000 go on to play in college, according to the most recent NCAA statistics. Although the number of athletes decreases drastically from high school to college, it is certainly not for lack of talent and trying. Learn all that you can to better your odds.

CHAPTER 5

FOOTBALL DIVISIONS (X)

About the Football Divisions

So you want to play college football, *ay?* At what level? What division? Do you know your options? Throughout the recruiting process, you could potentially speak with coaches at schools that you've never heard of, so it's great to be familiar with (or at least have baseline knowledge to apply when you hear) terms like DI, FCS, DII, DIII, and FBS. Always do your research!

Most college football starts and ends with the National Collegiate Athletics Association (NCAA). The NCAA is the governing body of not only college football, but most college sports as well. NCAA ensures that high school students meet certain qualifications in order to participate in playing sports. The NCAA is also responsible for the rules and regulations for each sport. They make sure that college coaches abide by the rules, especially with regards to recruiting.

NCAA

Division I

Football Bowl Subdivision (FBS)

The Football Bowl Subdivision consists of ten conferences divided into "Power 5" and "Group of 5" (mid-major) schools. FBS schools typically have the largest student bodies and athletic budgets. This means they will have larger crowds and more money to spend, so they will be able to provide the student-athletes and coaches more than other programs. FBS schools will have larger facilities and stadiums as well, meaning that their locker rooms, player lounges, and weight rooms will typically be larger than those of other universities.

Since the athletic budget is bigger, they can provide more gear, such as hats, socks, shirts, and shorts. They are also able to provide more snacks such as protein bars, shakes, fruits, and meals. They offer full-ride scholarships only, no partials, as well as cost of attendance checks (a.k.a. extra money) to football athletes.

FBS programs have the opportunity to participate in postseason bowl games. Bowl games are awarded to the teams that win at least six or more games based on their twelve-game schedule. FBS schools are bowl eligible when they when six games, and those six qualifying games have to be against other FBS programs. Players love bowl games for numerous reasons, but one in particular is the variety of bowl gifts that are given.

Bowl gifts range depending on the bowl caliber, but the gifts they usually offer are pretty unique. I was fortunate enough to go to

the New Orleans Bowl sponsored by R&L Carriers. As a coach, I
received gifts ranging from designer accessories to jewelry selected
from an amazing catalog. The most unique gift that players and
coaches could get was a reclining chair that the bowl game would
ship to a location of the recipient's choice. Other bowl games
offer video game consoles and Apple TVs. FCS schools and below
participate in a playoff system only. They do not participate in bowl
games, nor do they receive any gifts like FBS schools who go to
bowl games.

FBS schools with a big enough budgets will offer their players
what's called a training table. A training table is a selection of
handpicked food by the football staff. These meals are offered daily
for players and are usually all-you-can-eat buffet style. FCS schools
may cater meals for the team, but only every once in a while. Those
players primarily go to the cafeteria for their daily food intake. The
cafeteria is regulated by the school, while training table meals are
chosen by the football staff.

Let's not forget that FBS players also usually have more gear than
lower-level schools. This is why FBS schools are more attractive to
student-athletes than FCS or smaller football-budgeted schools.

Let's dive into the Power 5. As stated in the name, it consists of five
of the most popular and well-known conferences: the Atlantic Coast
Conference, the Southeastern Conference, the Big Ten Conference,
the Big 12 Conference, and the Pac 12 Conference. These schools
have the largest football budgets and are most recognizable due to
being on TV the most. Because of their larger fan bases, they are on
TV more often due to more people tuning in to watch.

Schools listed within each conference are located in the same
regions. So if you're located on the West Coast, you will likely be

more familiar with the Pac 12 schools. If you're located on the
East Coast, you will likely be more familiar with the Atlantic Coast
conference schools. See the chart below to view the schools listed in
each conference.

ATLANTIC COAST CONFERENCE:

Notre Dame, Clemson, Miami, North Carolina, North
Carolina State, Pitt, Virginia, Virginia Tech, Wake Forest,
Georgia Tech, Louisville, Florida State, Duke, Syracuse,
Boston College

SOUTHEASTERN CONFERENCE:

Florida, Georgia, Missouri, Kentucky, Tennessee, Vanderbilt,
South Carolina, Alabama, Texas A&M, Auburn, Ole Miss,
Mississippi State, LSU, Arkansas

BIG TEN CONFERENCE:

Ohio State, Indiana, Penn State, Maryland, Rutgers,
Michigan, Michigan State, Northwestern, Wisconsin, Iowa,
Minnesota, Nebraska, Purdue, Illinois

BIG 12 CONFERENCE:

Oklahoma, Iowa State, Texas, Oklahoma State, West
Virginia, TCU, Kansas State, Texas Tech, Kansas, Baylor

PAC 12 CONFERENCE:

Washington, Oregon, Stanford, Oregon State, UC Berkeley,
Washington State, USC, Colorado, Utah, UCLA, Arizona
State, Arizona

Mid-major schools, which are also known as the Group of 5, are next on the totem pole in regard to being the most popular and recognizable schools. There are five conferences. Mid-major programs don't have as big of a recruiting budget as Power 5 schools, but they still have a good budget to work with. These schools are comparable to some of the Power 5 schools, but not quite as big. Listed below are the Group of 5 conferences.

SUNBELT CONFERENCE:
Appalachian State, Georgia State, Georgia Southern, Troy, Coastal Carolina, Louisiana, Louisiana Monroe, Texas State, Texas at Arlington, Arkansas State, Arkansas at Little Rock, South Alabama

MID-AMERICAN CONFERENCE:
Buffalo, Kent State, Ohio, Miami (Ohio), Bowling Green, Akron, Ball State, Toledo, W. Michigan, Central Michigan, E. Michigan, Northern Illinois

CONFERENCE USA:
Marshall, FAU, Western Kentucky, UNC Charlotte, Middle Tennessee, FIU, UAB, UTSA, Louisiana Tech, North Texas, Rice, UTEP, Old Dominion, Southern Mississippi, UT El Paso

AMERICAN ATHLETIC CONFERENCE:
UCF, Temple, Cincinnati, USF, East Carolina, UConn, Memphis, Houston, Tulane, SMU, Navy, Tulsa

MOUNTAIN WEST CONFERENCE:
San Jose State, Boise State, Hawaii, Fresno State, Air Force, San Diego State, Colorado State, Wyoming, New Mexico, Utah State, UNLV, Nevada

Power 5 conference schools can only sign twenty-five scholarships annually. Here is an interesting thought to ponder: if a school were to sign twenty-five players a year, then in four years, a hundred total players could be on scholarship. However, there can actually only be eighty-five players on scholarship at a time. Tricky, huh? It is an unfortunate reality that every year, players leave the program for a variety of reasons. Technically, every four years, FBS schools should have at least one hundred players on scholarship, but players will end up leaving the program over a four-year-span. Every year, there are reports about players being dismissed from the football program for disciplinary reasons, failing out of school due to grades, or entering their names into what's called the transfer portal.

When a player decides to leave their current school to play elsewhere, they enter their names into the transfer portal. The transfer portal was established in 2018 to make it easier for players to move to different schools. Prior to this, a school could not legally contact another player until the compliance office and head coach of the player's current school signed off on a release. Since the transfer portal has been established for a while now, any player can enter the transfer portal at any time without notifying their current coach. All they have to do is contact the compliance office and tell them they want to transfer, and their names will be placed in the portal.

I encourage any player considering a transfer to have a conversation with their coach prior to entering the portal. A reminder: it is critical to do as much research on schools you're interested in up front so you can avoid this situation. Transferring schools can be a very difficult and uncertain process. There is no guarantee that a player will get a scholarship from another school when they enter their name into the portal. There is a tremendous amount of risk when players decide to go into the portal.

There have been some very alarming numbers that have surfaced since the transfer portal was established. Since 2018, there have been 1,086 players who have entered the portal. Of that total, 189 have transferred, 856 have not transferred, and 41 withdrew from the portal. Basically, 189 players successfully transferred out of 1,086. These numbers are the way they are because every year, there is a recruiting class coming in between high school and JUCO. There are also walk-ons at these schools who have worked hard to earn spots. Coaches will put these players on scholarship rather than going out to get an uncertain product out of the portal. Then, there is a ton of competition in the transfer portal itself. Please keep in mind that, as prevalent as they may seem, scholarships are extremely hard to come by.

A former recruit with whom I built a good relationship decided to give me a call and ask for my thoughts about him getting into the transfer portal. I proceeded to ask him if he was on full scholarship. He said yes. Out of curiosity, I asked him if the coaches had mistreated him or done him wrong in any way. He said no. I asked him how much he had played since he had been at the school. He said not very much. My advice to him was to stay put at that school and keep pushing.

I gave him this advice because at whatever school any player decides to attend, there will be adversity and discomfort that must be overcome. I remember reading this book by a pastor I greatly respect by the name of T.D. Jakes. In this book, he mentions the "eighty-twenty rule." The eighty-twenty rule has been very eye-opening for me. He talks about how nothing in life will ever be perfect, mainly because nobody is perfect (ourselves included).

Thus, if 80 percent of something is good, then you should keep rolling with it. He talks about how many people will focus on the 20 percent that is negative and give up the 80 percent that's good. So based on the questions I asked the young man, it appeared that 80 percent of his situation was favorable, but he was willing to risk giving that up for the missing 20 percent.

My point in this story is that players should always evaluate why they are choosing to enter the transfer portal. You could very well be forfeiting a *full-ride scholarship*! It is a very big deal to graduate from college with no debt. This young man was very young in his college career. It was not worth risking a full-ride scholarship in his situation. As always, I left the decision up to him, but my thoughts were very clear: stay your butt in school, get your degree, outwork everybody there, and ball out on the field.

Recruits, keep in mind that at every position, there will be multiple players who coaches are willing to take commitments from (not just you).

> Any player who has a committable offer can call and commit at any time. Understand that while you're waiting, your spot could be taken by another offered player. There are only a small number of spots to fill each year.

Football Champion Subdivision (FCS)

The Football Championship Subdivision has fourteen conferences and 127 schools. FCS football schools can offer sixty-three full athletic scholarships annually. These sixty-three scholarships can be divided among eighty-five players. FCS schools play a twelve-game schedule, and based on their record, they have an opportunity to play in the playoffs. FCS schools don't participate in bowl games; rather, they have a playoff system.

Additionally:

- Ivy League schools are considered Division I-AA (FCS), but do not offer athletic scholarships and do not have a postseason.
- Historically Black Colleges and Universities (HBCUs) are considered Division I-AA (FCS), offer full scholarships, and participate in bowl games.

Division II

There are seventeen Division II football conferences and 169 Division II schools. Division II schools offer thirty-six partial athletic scholarships only.

Division III

Division III has twenty-nine conferences and 250 football schools. Division III offers *no* athletic scholarships (only academic and need-based), and Division III football is the largest of all athletic divisions. Division III football schools have a postseason playoff system, and they don't play in bowl games.

National Junior College Athletic Association (NJCAA)

Junior college (JUCO) offers full athletic scholarships annually (which can be divided into partial scholarships). JUCOs in some states offer football, but no athletic scholarships. The number of scholarships varies by institution. JUCO schools participate in bowl games, and there are 136 football schools at this level.

National Association of Intercollegiate Athletics (NAIA)

The ninety-six NAIA football schools offer twenty-four athletic scholarships annually that can also be divided into partial scholarships per team. NAIA schools participate in the playoff system and are not bowl game eligible.

CHAPTER 6

STAR RATINGS & RECRUITING TIERS (O)

Each year, you'll see football prospects get excited about receiving their star rating. Once they do, they post them on social media and their Hudl film for all to see. Let's delve into that.

The major recruiting services—247Sports, Rivals, and ESPN— have scouts and analysts who review prospects by using a scale/ composite score to add star ratings that convey the talent level of a specific recruit. Star ratings range from two to five stars. Star ratings are subjective, and ratings can vary depending on which source or website you reference. There is no one-star rating offered.

While star ratings are *all the rage* among high school athletes and many sports writers, college coaches *do not recruit* based on stars. Star ratings are for fans and media who follow college football closely, but they do matter to a certain extent. Some football programs will receive bonuses based on the rankings of the recruiting class they bring in.

College football coaches understand that no matter how many stars you have in a recruiting class, it's all about the win-and-loss column in the fall football season. For this reason, coaches recruit based on film. How good the player's film is determines their recruitment. Your film is what matters most in terms of getting the attention of college recruiters and football coaches. A player with a two-star rating and great film can absolutely make it onto college recruiting boards, so be sure to show up on your film.

Here's a typical priority breakdown:

- Five- and four-star recruits are players who have national offers from schools across the country and are always top priority.
- Three-star recruits with Power 5 offers who will attend Power 5 schools are next in priority.
- Three-star recruits who have mid-major offers are a bit lower, but these players are borderline Power 5 athletes. They may have one or two Power 5 offers that are not committable.
- Two- and three-star recruits who will all only have mid-major offers are next.
- Two- and three-star recruits who will have FCS committable offers, with a few mid-major offers that may or may not be committable, are last in priority.

Knowing where you stack up in recruitment tiers can help you make a better decision. Otherwise, you could be waiting for an offer that will never come. If you have committable mid-major offers and no Power 5 offers by July or August going into your senior year, I would seriously consider committing to a mid-major. Trust me, the NFL will find you wherever you play.

Every NFL team has a department that scouts for talent. Their full-time job is to search high and low to find and scout talent across the United States. Whether you are playing at an FBS school or at an NAIA school, the scouts will find you. It is their job to find talent at every level of football. While I did not play FBS football, I did play JUCO and FCS football. Even without the FBS or Power 5 tag, I got drafted in the 2010 NFL draft. Let's remember to maintain our focus. The goal here is to earn a scholarship and play college football first and foremost.

When I was recruited to the University of Central Arkansas, there was a former player who had been drafted by the Tennessee Titans. When I arrived on campus, there was a freshman I played with who would go on to get drafted by the New England Patriots. Once I got drafted by the Jacksonville Jaguars, the very next year I was teammates with a player named Cecil Shorts. Cecil Shorts was from a Division III school. Another great teammate of mine in Jacksonville was Rashean Mathis, a Pro Bowler and HBCU graduate. The list goes on and on, so go where you are wanted and make big plays.

FBS schools are obviously great, and they definitely have amenities that are most favorable to student-athletes. The point here is that I absolutely enjoyed my FCS collegiate playing experience and earned a degree. I would have loved for my junior college to have a training table, or for TV network deals that allowed me to play on ESPN every weekend. It did not have those things, but what it did have was a great opportunity to get a free education and continue to pursue my dreams while playing college football.

What makes the college experience so great is the relationships with the coaches and players you are going to be around for the next four years, and those relationships will continue to prove genuine well into your adulthood. Some relationships you develop in college will last the rest of your life.

Every recruit's situation is different, so be sure to go for a school based on your unique situation. What are your chances of getting on the field for playing time? Does the school really want you, or is it more that you really want the school? Is proximity to home and your family's ability to attend games and see you play important to you? While at Holmes Community College, I coached a player who transferred from a Power 5 school. He left the Power 5 school because he was unhappy there and didn't like the relationships that he had with his coaches. Therefore, he decided to go to junior college to start his recruiting process over again and try to attend a different school.

While I was on staff at Arkansas State University, there was a player who transferred from a premier college football programs to Arkansas State. I remember his reasoning was that he had been there for three years and could not touch the field. He could not get any playing time because he had future NFL players starting in front of him. He was able to transfer to Arkansas State University, get on the field almost immediately, and receive significant playing time.

During my time at the University of South Alabama, I recruited this player from Florida who decided to go to a Power 5 school, and one year later he decided that he was too far from home and not getting any significant playing time. He wanted his family to be able to attend games and see him play, so he transferred to the University of South Alabama, a smaller school that met his needs.

On paper, and when coming out of JUCO, I personally had better schools to choose from than the University of Central Arkansas, but I decided in my gut that it was the best fit for me.

The different stories are endless; a player's needs, wants, and priorities change. It is very common to hear stories about players who are unhappy about the college they have chosen. With that in mind, choose a school as wisely as you can and with your specific needs in mind. Do your best to not end up in the transfer portal later. If a coach truly wants you, they'll be more invested in you being a good football player, as well as in your future beyond football. While some are fancier than others, every football program in America has a sufficient weight room and sports facilities. Best advice: go where you are wanted!

Final Thoughts: No matter how many stars you have, you could end up on the bench. Practice a little humility and never fall into the trap of thinking you're "better than" a scholarship offer you've been presented. While most high school players dream of clutching that big SEC offer, keep in mind that sometimes it's hard for five-star recruits to stand out or make a splash when stacked against other five-star recruits on the depth chart. I'm sure you are already aware, but I must drive home the point that any school that offers you a full ride, so you can play the game that you love debt-free, is a blessing. Furthermore, if you are putting up numbers and making a big splash at a DIII school, the NFL will find you. *I cannot emphasize that enough.* Ball out and be humble!

CONVERSATION STARTERS:

1. What are some things to consider when choosing a school and football program after high school?
2. Who will help you make the decision on what school to attend?
3. What steps are you taking to reach your ideal school?
4. If your ideal school is not an option, what adjustments will you need to make?

HUDDLE UP: SECTION REVIEW

☐   What key takeaways and new information have you learned
    in this chapter?

    _____

    _____

    _____

    _____

☐   How has this chapter made you rethink or adjust your plan
    for recruitment?

    _____

    _____

    _____

    _____

Part II

KICK-OFF—X

CHAPTER 7

1ST & 10—NINTH GRADE (O)

Welcome to high school! With that, you've got a clean slate and a chance to set yourself up for a win, fresh out of the gate. It is extremely important for you to know at this moment that every grade you complete will count toward college. Getting accepted into to college requires a minimum GPA that you must achieve, and this is where your grades will start counting for NCAA academic requirements as well.

> **"THE SECRET TO GETTING AHEAD IS GETTING STARTED."**
> **—MARK TWAIN**

Have you heard of the saying "ignorance is bliss"? That was me, the clueless freshman. When I was in ninth grade, I had absolutely no clue what the NCAA was or even what a GPA truly meant. Please do not judge me. The only thing on my mind was playing football after school and keeping up with my chores around the house. I did not take my grades seriously and had a very lackadaisical approach. At my high school, they separated the ninth grade football team from the tenth to twelfth graders on the varsity football team. I played offensive tackle on the ninth grade team with no plan or vision to play college football. I was literally just living in the (oblivious) moment and taking it day by day.

I had no clue how important my grades were, or that ninth grade is an extremely important year and an excellent opportunity to start strong. However, I do remember having one conversation with my oldest brother and mentor, Ken, that was extremely pivotal to my football career. He encouraged me to play on the defensive side of the ball. He told me to go and ask the coaches about moving to linebacker. Although I am not entirely sure what made him instruct me to do this, I believe that he knew I wouldn't grow to be three hundred pounds and that an offensive position wouldn't fit my frame. He played on the defensive side of the ball both in high school and at Samford University, and I think he believed that would be a better fit for me. I did just that and they eventually moved me to defensive end, which I thought was just as good as playing linebacker, and "the rest is history."

When discussing GPAs with recruits, I hear countless stories about how they "didn't take their ninth or tenth grade years seriously," much like my own mindset at the time. And they pay for that later by needing to play catch-up. Same as I tell the outside linebackers in pass rush, "It all starts with your get-off."

Fun football fact: When a quarterback drops back to pass the ball, there are defensive ends and outside linebackers who are trying to tackle him to the ground. When I am coaching pass rushers, the number one thing I tell them is that it's all about their "get-off," meaning how fast the player moves toward the quarterback when the ball is snapped. It should happen simultaneously. When you hit the ninth grade, the hypothetical ball is snapped and it is extremely important that you "get off" to a great start.

Please understand that not taking ninth grade seriously can come back to haunt you and potentially keep you from getting to the college of your dreams. Transitioning to high school is a big deal, but don't take your grades lightly here as a freshman. If academics are not a factor holding you back, you will be very glad to be in a good position to go to the school of your choice.

At this stage, as a ninth grader, your position may change due to the fact that your body is still maturing and developing. Like I mentioned earlier, I went from an offensive lineman in youth sports to being a pass rushing defensive end in college. With that in mind, it is important to develop your skills and grow as a football player.

LEARN THE BASIC FUNDAMENTALS OF FOOTBALL NOW BY LEARNING HOW TO:

- Backpedal
- Move in space by flipping your hips
- Play with leverage (or play low)
- Tackle with proper technique

For instance, if you are a running back, practice running routes or running the football. What is important at this stage is to get out, play football, and work on drills as much as possible. You are so young as a freshman, and it is early in the recruiting process, so what is important to do at this point is develop your body and work on how to move it correctly.

SO HERE'S THE PLAY:

- ☐ Read through the ninth grade plan
- ☐ Prioritize your academics and focus on grades
- ☐ Begin ACT/SAT prep

- ☐ Continue team building
- ☐ Establish your online presence
- ☐ Add extra skills
- ☐ Visit schools of interest online via virtual visits and in person when available
- ☐ Plan your summer training
- ☐ Schedule an end-of-year academic meeting

➔ **REVIEW EACH DETAIL OF THIS NINTH GRADE PLAN (BELOW) WITH YOUR PARENTS.**

Get your parents/guardians on board, first. It's important to review the steps here and edit as needed to suit your wants and needs. As your biggest supporters, your parents can best help you on your journey when they are aware of the plan to execute. Have a talk. Are they in agreement? Discuss changes. Ask them for input. Parents should educate themselves and help their student-athletes navigate the NCAA Eligibility Center (also known as the NCAA Clearinghouse) requirements to participate in collegiate athletics.

WHAT IS THE NCAA ELIGIBILITY CENTER?

The NCAA Eligibility Center certifies whether prospective college athletes are eligible to play sports at NCAA Division I or II institutions. It does this by reviewing the student-athlete's academic record, SAT or ACT scores, and academic status to ensure conformity with NCAA rules.

We will discuss more specifics on the NCAA Eligibility Center in the next chapter. Reviewing your plan with your biggest fans shows you're intent on success and committed to your future.

➜ **PRIORITIZE YOUR ACADEMICS & FOCUS ON GRADES!**

Start by introducing yourself to your guidance counselor (a.k.a. your brand-new teammate) and let them know your goal of playing football at the collegiate level. Send an email (preferably the summer before entering ninth grade) to make an appointment for a meeting. Your parents can help you set this up and should also attend. *See, you're team building here!* The discussion should include checking your current class registration as it pertains to qualifying for NCAA and high school graduation requirements. After speaking with your parents, you may also want to discuss the potential to become an early enrollee your senior year. I know it seems early to think about your senior year, but trust me, the time will fly by. If you don't have a plan already in place, you may not have the option if you decide that it's beneficial later.

WHAT IS AN EARLY ENROLLEE?

An enrollee is a signee who graduates high school in December instead of May and attends college as a student-athlete in January.

Why enroll early? Aside from being more appealing to college coaches, being an early enrollee (also referred to as a "Greenshirt" athlete) signals to coaches that you're an academically sound student who takes care of business. If all things are dead-even in player recruitment regarding grades, test scores, athleticism, and ability among recruits, the early enrollee will typically get the nod and beat out their competition. Graduating high school in December instead of May can be beneficial as it allows the student-athlete to participate with a college team during spring football, bowl and playoff practices, and could help put them in a better position to earn playing time as a college freshman. Typically, high school kids can become early enrollees by taking extra classes during the summer to earn credits faster. You can also go to your guidance counselor to discuss more options, virtual school options, or flexible scheduling to allow for early high school graduation.

While I was coaching at the University of South Alabama, I received a commitment from a player who was an early enrollee and was going to have the ability to enroll in college for the spring term. There have been notable early enrollees in Power 5 programs as well. Tua Tagovailoa and Jalen Hurts are both former early enrollees that are currently playing on NFL rosters.

Not that important to you? *Okay.* Next question... Do you plan on earning a master's degree in college? Early enrollees get a head start on their college courses and typically finish their bachelor's degree early, allowing them the opportunity to also earn a master's degree (around twenty-four extra collegiate hours or so) with their athletic scholarship. Additionally, can you go back and attend your senior prom and graduation? Typically, yes! Seems like the best of both worlds to me. But *I digress*—back to the academics.

Pro Tip: As a freshman in high school, and before you set foot in a single class, you need to know that your grade record starts now, and NCAA-qualifying GPAs are based solely on the grades you earn in your core classes.

CORE CLASSES = ENGLISH, MATH, SCIENCE, HISTORY, AND FOREIGN LANGUAGE

Elective classes are not included in GPA calculations for NCAA eligibility. Electives are needed for high school graduation. Student-athletes need to meet both high school graduation and NCAA requirements to qualify. Be careful with your course choices: you can graduate from high school and still not qualify to play college football.

Pro Tip: Every high school has a 48H form that lists the qualifying high school courses for the NCAA. Ask your guidance counselor or find the list at www.eligibiltycenter.org.

THE CORE COURSES NEEDED TO QUALIFY FOR THE NCAA LOOK SOMETHING LIKE THIS:

- ☐ Four years of English
- ☐ Three years of math (algebra 1 or higher)
- ☐ Two years of natural/physical science (including one year of lab science if your high school offers it)
- ☐ One additional year of English, math, or natural/ physical science
- ☐ Two years of social science
- ☐ Four additional years of English, math, natural/physical science, social science, foreign language, comparative religion, or philosophy

→   **BEGIN ACT/SAT TEST PREP.**

Get tutoring and other study help to begin crafting better test-taking skills. Those skills will help you in your core classes, as well as on your upcoming college entrance exams. Check your local community programs and local organizations for what prep classes are being offered after school and on weekends. Your guidance counselor should have a list.

→   **CONTINUE TEAM BUILDING.**

Developing good relationships with your "team" is so important. High school teachers, coaches, trainers, school administrators, and support staff should be your biggest allies. Show them that you are a good teammate. Not sure what that looks like?

HERE'S A GLIMPSE:

☐ Work hard.
☐ Be on time.
☐ Complete your schoolwork.
☐ Don't miss workouts.
☐ Ask for help.
☐ Stay after class.
☐ Show good character traits and start building a
     solid reputation.

Athletes typically have a *school-wide reputation*, so be sure yours is top notch! Coaches will ask around about you.

➜ **ESTABLISH YOUR ONLINE PRESENCE.**

Fun Fact: Twitter is the most popular social media platform among coaches for the recruitment of players. It's extremely rare to find a coach who is not utilizing Twitter for recruitment. Nick Saban may actually be the only one, because he doesn't need it.

FBS (Group of 5 tier) schools and below do not typically have the budget to go all in on nationwide recruiting—they usually stay within a six-hour radius of the school. But they will "spot recruit" for a good prospect outside of that as needed. So solidifying your online presence and reaching out to coaches will help your recruitment and increase your chances of receiving a full ride.

Pro Tip: Your Twitter profile should be easy to find and match your real name. It can be quite difficult for coaches to find John Johnson whose Twitter handle is @jjohnbandzzz for obvious reasons.

A bad example of a Twitter bio is one that does not include any information regarding the player stats. I see some Twitter bios from recruits that might say, "The official Twitter page of JJ Johnson... NO CEILINGS," and nothing more. There is no other stat, film link, or player information provided. This usually signifies that the player considers himself so great that they can easily be Googled. And while that may be the case, it's never a good idea to make recruiting coaches hunt for you in a sea of hungry recruits. That is one of the fastest ways to get overlooked or bypassed altogether.

IN YOUR TWITTER BIO, INCLUDE:

- ☐ Your Hudl link
- ☐ Height and weight
- ☐ School and state
- ☐ Position
- ☐ Graduation class
- ☐ Forty-yard dash time
- ☐ If you're a multi-sport athlete

IN YOUR TWITTER POSTS, INCLUDE:

- ☐ Workout and in-game clips (some workout examples include dunking, power cleans, box jumps, quick ladders, cone drills, and fieldwork)
- ☐ Awards and accolades
- ☐ Anything that showcases your academic and physical ability

Pro Tip: Be careful what you post—coaches will view your profile and shy away from recruits who post, retweet, and like distasteful things. That's also very subjective, so be careful. For example, I have seen players like or retweet sexually inappropriate behavior. I have also seen players record videos of themselves smoking and/or vaping, and whether the substance is illegal or legal, it is never a good look and should always be avoided. Players have lost scholarships based on negative things (or even the appearance of these) posted on social media.

➜ ADD EXTRA SKILLS.

As a player, you want to add all of the extra skills you can to make yourself marketable. One of the most quietly coveted skills is long snapping. Long snapping is very valuable because it can have an impact on the outcome of a game. If there is a bad snap during a game, it counts as a turnover and will give the other team momentum. Many teams will offer scholarships to great long snappers with no questions asked. Look it up—the NFL is included in the long snapper love. It is a highly sought after, unique skill position in the football industry. Start practicing to become great at it now, and when you do, *add it to your Hudl film.*

Are you a teen creative? Due to the popularity of social media, graphics and video skills are a hot commodity everywhere, and this includes athletic programs across the nation. Can you make the kind of football graphics you see floating all over Twitter and other platforms? Can you create and edit great team highlight videos? Trust me, the team needs you, and although it's an off-the-field role, scholarships can be earned in this area. Tell a friend to tell a friend. (More on this in chapter 11.)

➜ START ATTENDING FOOTBALL GAMES AT SCHOOLS OF INTEREST.

Check out the "game day atmosphere."

Pro Tip: Join an older player who is currently being recruited on their campus visit, if possible. This will give you an idea of what to expect.

➜ GET YOUR SUMMER TRAINING LINED UP WITH A
SEVEN-ON-SEVEN TEAM.

WHAT IS A SEVEN-ON-SEVEN TEAM?

A seven-on-seven team is composed of players who are
local to an area. These teams compete against other seven-
on-seven teams in their state during the off-season. Teams
typically compete before high school spring football begins,
as well as during the summer months. No helmets, pads, or
tackling are involved in seven-on-seven play. Players join
these teams primarily to expand their network. Seven-on-
seven participation also allows players to showcase their
talent and football development.

WHY JOIN A SEVEN-ON-SEVEN TEAM?

Many of these coaches have relationships and rapport with
college coaches, which helps your networking ability. Seven-
on-seven coaches also typically take groups of recruits to
college campuses for summer camps and unofficial visits.

Start building relationships with local seven-on-seven coaches for
summer training. Be sure to get connected with the right seven-on-
seven team. It's about exposure here. You'll compete against other
players and see how you measure up, which could also help you
with recruiting. Does the coach have a history of players signing
scholarships to play college football? Not sure? Ask the older
players who are currently being recruited about their experiences.

Keep the lines of communication open between you, your high school coach, and your seven-on-seven coach.

➜ **SCHEDULE AN END-OF-YEAR ACADEMIC MEETING.**

At the end of the year (May/June), schedule a quick academic check-in with your guidance counselor. Depending on when your final grades post, this may be an email. Hopefully, you'll have been tracking your grades all year, and you'll know if you have an academic issue. But if you haven't, it never hurts to ask. Again, don't leave anything up to chance.

Ask your counselor: "Do I need to retake or replace any grades in my core classes?" If so, ask to be enrolled in your district or state virtual program to replace or recover any and all Ds or Fs that are currently on your transcript in your core classes. We want As and Bs, always!

If you are considering the early enrollment option, please discuss and revisit the plan with your counselor annually.

➜ **HAVE A GREAT SUMMER!**

On top of your high school summer workout requirements and seven-on-seven team participation, remember to keep building good habits and continue to "Separate Yourself"—refer back to that chapter often.

HUDDLE UP: SECTION REVIEW

☐   What key takeaways and new information have you learned
     in this chapter?

     _____

     _____

     _____

     _____

☐   How has reading this chapter changed the way you are
     thinking of approaching your first year of high school?

     _____

     _____

     _____

     _____

CHAPTER 8

2ND DOWN—TENTH GRADE (X)

During my tenth grade year, I was happy to get some playing time on the high school varsity team! I was developing into a player the coaches could depend upon. I still had no clue about my academic standing and what I needed to do academically to continue playing football. I didn't talk to my guidance counselor or my parents about grades, but I was eligible to play varsity sports, and I thought that was good enough. It wasn't. Honestly, I really did not have any aspirations of playing college football at this point. I didn't have a plan whatsoever—I was just going with the flow, enjoying putting on my number 91 jersey on game days. Thankfully, you have *The Recruit's Playbook* in hand, a roadmap to follow, and vision. You're leaps and bounds ahead of where I was at this stage of the game.

So now that you have a full year of *The Recruit's Playbook* and core grades under your belt, it's time for a quick self-assessment of your performance. How did you do last year? Preview the next phase of your plan with your parents. In what areas do you need improvement, to hit reset, and/or make adjustments? Let's get after it!

HERE'S THE PLAY:

☐ Read through the tenth grade plan
☐ Register with the NCAA Eligibility Center

☐ Prioritize your academics and focus on grades

☐ Continue ACT/SAT prep

☐ Update your Hudl film and Twitter bio stats

☐ Continue building your brand

☐ Visit schools of interest

☐ Schedule an end-of-year academic meeting

☐ Go to summer football camps

➔ **REGISTER WITH THE NCAA ELIGIBILITY CENTER AND CREATE A FREE PROFILE PAGE AT WWW. ELIGIBILITYCENTER.ORG.**

Every recruit will have to register with the NCAA Eligibility Center in order to submit their academic records, so it's better to go ahead and set up your account now to take care of this step.

Write down your login info.

Check your account periodically for next steps and NCAA updates.

➔ **PRIORITIZE YOUR ACADEMICS AND FOCUS ON GRADES!**

Grade Check: You must have a minimum core GPA of 2.3 to be a full qualifier. For example: If you made all Cs last year in your core classes, you only have a 2.0 GPA and are currently an NCAA non-qualifier.

Meet with your guidance counselor. A student, parent, and guidance counselor meeting is ideal. Make sure you are on track to graduate, discuss your core GPA, and check for any necessary academic changes and/or grade replacements needed.

Mediocre and poor grades (Cs, Ds, and Fs) in core academic classes can cost you major (scholarship) money. For every C you earn in a core class, you'll need an A or B to balance it. If you earn a D, then you'll need an A to balance it. Elective classes such as art and weightlifting cannot save you.

Reminder: Elective grades are removed from your GPA calculations by the NCAA.

Teachers are your teammates! Approach your classes with the intent to succeed. Don't just show up. Be prepared to dominate. Do your absolute best in your course enrollments. If you find yourself struggling, do something about it. Stay after class, meet with teachers, attend their study sessions, and seek the extra help you need.

PARENT PRO TIP:

Hold your student-athlete accountable. Check on their classes and grades often (and especially at each nine-week grading period). Report cards matter!

➜ **CONTINUE YOUR ACT/SAT TEST PREP.**

Get tutoring and join study groups to help you improve in your classes and on your upcoming exams.

→ **UPDATE YOUR HUDL FILM AND STATS IN YOUR TWITTER BIO AS NEEDED.**

Keep your Hudl link, height and weight, school and state, position, graduation class, forty-yard dash time, and multi-sport athlete status up to date.

Remember: On Hudl, arrange your best (and most explosive) plays *first*!

How's your long snapping practice going? (See "Add Extra Skills" from last year's plan on page 95.)

→ **KEEP BUILDING YOUR BRAND.**

Follow coaches on social media and make face-to-face introductions with the coaches recruiting your school. That's a major key!

Typically, the coaches who visit your school most often are recruiting all of the local talent in your area. On recruiting visits, your high school coach will be asked about each player's character, attitude, love of football, academics, familial situation, and coachability, among other things. The feedback received will greatly impact player recruitment. College coaches know the demands of playing college football are difficult, so they are looking for young men who have a strong character, because they will otherwise struggle to try and make it in college football.

I was once recruiting a player out of a JUCO with really good film. He had great size and speed. Obviously, based on film, we wanted to offer this young man a scholarship. It was no-brainer. However, when I called his coach, he told me that the kid was not reliable

and had a poor attitude. He said that the player was extremely
talented but was a bad teammate. I decided to stop recruiting
this player, because ultimately this could have a negative impact
on our program, and no team needs that. With that information
being consistent with a few other reports on this player, I moved
on to the next recruit. Be mindful that—I cannot stress this
enough—behavior, attitude, and character are key factors in
player recruitment.

If you get the opportunity, accompany an older player who is
currently being recruited on their "Junior Day" campus visit. This
will allow you to potentially gain exposure and possibly meet (in
person) coaches that you haven't yet met or have reached out
to virtually.

➜ SCHEDULE AN END-OF-YEAR ACADEMIC MEETING.

At the end of the year (May/June), schedule a quick academic
check-in with your guidance counselor. Depending on when your
final grades post, this may be an email. Hopefully, you'll have
been tracking your grades all year, and you'll know if you have an
academic issue. But if you haven't, or just want to be sure, it never
hurts to ask.

Ask your counselor: "Do I need to retake or replace any grades
in my core classes?" If so, ask to be enrolled in your district or state
virtual program, or other options to replace or recover any and all
Ds or Fs that are currently on your transcript in your core classes.
Be sure to have your counselor check the 48H form to be sure the
course will count, as some grade recovery courses do not.

*If you are considering the early enrollment option, please revisit
the plan with your counselor annually.*

➔ GO TO SUMMER FOOTBALL CAMPS.

At football camps, coaches encounter young players who may show great ability and potential but move like newborn fawns. Their bodies do not move properly when running drills, and/or some movements appear awkward simply because the players are still developing the proper motor skills needed for football. These players are not yet comfortable with the complex body positions football requires. It is important at this stage (ninth and tenth grade) to get out and play football as much as you can. Continually do drills to help your body mature. Football is a very complex sport in regard to movement. You must combine explosion, power, and speed with balance and *finesse*. This takes a lot of practice.

Attending football camps and performing well is key to continue building your brand and gaining experience. On top of your high school summer workout requirements and seven-on-seven team participation, remember to keep building good habits and continue to "Separate Yourself."

Pro Tip: Go to one-day camps at schools that are currently showing you the most interest and are also on your "top pick" list. Trust me, I get it. The lure of attending mega-camps at big name schools is real, but choose wisely as it can be difficult to stand out, be noticed, and get offers among the masses of talented athletes in attendance.

CONVERSATION STARTERS:

1. In two to three sentences, explain the quotes below from *The Recruit's Playbook* in your own words:
   - "The secret to getting ahead is getting started."
   - "Tough times don't last. Tough people do."
   - "If you really want to do it, you do it. There are no excuses."

2. True/False: The grades you earn in elective courses are removed from your GPA calculations by the NCAA. _____

3. Fill-in-the-Blank: NCAA qualifying GPAs are based solely on the grades you earn in your _____ classes. You can speak to your guidance counselor and find the classes that qualify on your school's ____
_____.

4. You must graduate with _____
_____ total core credits for NCAA eligibility.

5. Many student-athletes have a "school-wide reputation." What is a reputation? How does your reputation affect your recruitment?

6. You must have a minimum core GPA of _____ to be a full NCAA qualifier. What is your current core GPA? How can you improve it?

7. Once you receive your ACT/SAT test results, match them with your core-course GPA on the NCAA Division I _____. If you have a low core-course GPA, you need higher test scores to be eligible. Do you need a higher core GPA, test score, or both to qualify?

HUDDLE UP: SECTION REVIEW

☐ What key takeaways and new information have you learned
   in this chapter?

   _____

   _____

   _____

   _____

☐ How did planning during your ninth grade year set you up
   for success in the tenth grade?

   _____

   _____

   _____

   _____

☐ What can you do now to make next year even better?

   _____

   _____

   _____

   _____

CHAPTER 9

3RD & SHORT—
ELEVENTH GRADE (O)

During my eleventh grade year, I became more aware of playing college football, and my aspirations started to build. I was a native Mississippian who loved all of the Florida teams as a high school athlete. The University of Miami, the University of Florida, and Florida State University were my favorites. However, I still had no awareness of what it took to be a qualifier to play college football at any level, especially at a Power 5 school. As a junior, I finally decided that I wanted to play college football at a Power 5 school, and then go on to play in the NFL.

I was a starter my eleventh grade year, and I was one of the better players on the team. Deep down, I knew that there was another level I could get to in my game. I knew that I had not reached my full potential athletically, but I couldn't quite tap into whatever I needed to push myself and my play to the highest gear. This was evident because the game of football was always so slow to me. I understood exactly what I needed to do on the field, but I didn't play fast and relentlessly at this point. I knew I had it in me, and I showed my talent, but my effort, grit, and tenacity were mediocre. I never really laid it all on the line.

Additionally, my academics were still subpar (with no dedicated ACT or SAT test prep or tests taken yet), and I still had not set foot in my high school guidance counselor's office at this point.

Yep, I was doing it all wrong. But congratulations—*you* are prepared and focused. This will not be your high school recruitment reality (nightmare).

We're closing in on our target. I told you the time would fly by! This year, like every other, is important to your future goal of playing collegiate football, only at this point, the finish line is just one year away. We've got less time to fix mistakes and make adjustments. As we coaches say to players on game day, if you weren't before, it's time to get locked in!

HERE'S THE PLAY:

☐ Read through the eleventh grade plan

☐ Register to take the Fall ACT and SAT

☐ Prioritize your academics and focus on grades

☐ Update your NCAA Eligibility Center profile page

☐ Continue ACT/SAT prep

☐ Update your Hudl film and Twitter bio stats

☐ Continue building your brand

☐ Schedule campus visits

☐ Schedule an end-of-year academic meeting

☐ Go to summer football camps

➜ PRIORITIZE YOUR ACADEMICS AND FOCUS ON GRADES (ALWAYS)!

Grade Check: Meet with your counselor (and bring a thank-you note) to make sure you will graduate on time with the required number of NCAA core courses. Check for any mistakes in your registration or on your transcripts.

Remember: You must have a minimum core GPA of 2.3 to be a full qualifier.

Teachers are your teammates! Meet with them, share your concerns, attend study sessions, do your absolute best in your course enrollments, and seek the extra help you need. I cannot reiterate enough how crucial it is for students to self-advocate. Speak up—this is important! That fully preventable D or F in a class should *not* stand in the way of your future.

➜ **REGISTER AND TAKE THE FIRST FALL ACT AND SAT TESTS OFFERED.**

Yes, I recommend taking both on your first attempt! Try out the different test formats and see with which one you feel more comfortable. You can submit your scores to the NCAA using code 9999.

Once you receive your fall test results, you'll know if a retake is needed. Check your SAT combined score or ACT sum score and match it to your core-course GPA on the Division I sliding scale.

DID YOU NAIL IT ON YOUR FIRST TRY?

- If you have a low test score, you need a higher core-course GPA to be eligible. If you have a low core-course GPA, you need a higher test score to be eligible.
- Not a great test taker? Get your core GPA as high as you possibly can. (See the importance of replacing those low grades in the summer.)

Pro Tip: Register for ACT/SAT retakes as needed. Retakes are not uncommon. Choose the test format (ACT or SAT) that you performed best on to retake. Do not miss the registration deadline. Continue your test prep and study groups for the next opportunity.

➡ CHECK YOUR NCAA ELIGIBILITY CENTER PROFILE PAGE AT: WWW.ELIGIBILITYCENTER.ORG.

Be sure that your sports participation information is added and correct on your account.

➡ UPDATE YOUR HUDL FILM AND BIO ON TWITTER.

Most players will begin picking up offers based on their junior season film, so make sure your film is great and ball out! Remember to add your most explosive plays from your junior season to Hudl.

Update your bio and stats on Twitter. Is your long snapping good enough to be added to your Hudl film? At this point, college coaches want to see the best plays of your junior season.

➡ KEEP BUILDING YOUR BRAND AND TAKE COLLEGE VISITS.

OFFICIAL VS. UNOFFICIAL VISITS

Any visit to a college campus by a college-bound student-athlete and/or their parents paid for by the college is an official visit. Visits paid for by student-athletes or their parents are unofficial visits.

Official visit invitations mean that schools are extremely interested in you. College recruiters will contact you about setting up an official visit. If you're in contact with a recruiter, then you can ask about setting up an unofficial visit; official visits are usually reserved for the priority recruits that colleges want to get committed. During an *official visit*, the college can pay for transportation to and from the college for the prospect, lodging, and three meals per day for the prospect and the parent or guardian, as well as *reasonable* entertainment expenses (including three tickets to a home sports event).

The only expenses a college-bound student-athlete may receive from a college during an *unofficial visit* are three tickets to a home sports event.

- **Fall:** Attend games at your schools of interest to check out the "game day atmosphere" and chat with coaches. Check out the schemes they are currently running and get a better feel for your potential future home.
- **Post-Junior Season (Jan/Feb):** Recruiting services can be quite expensive, and coaches must contend with limited to no-contact "dead periods" when they may not initiate contact with student-athletes. You can save money and give yourself a leg up by taking charge of your self-promotion and marketing.

Pro Tip: There are 254 DI and DI-AA schools in the country. I recommend sending 254 emails. It costs you nothing, and if you hear back from twenty schools and get three offers, that's a win! Remember to keep your options open and email lower divisions for scholarship opportunities as well. Draft a short email (or send a postcard) including the information from your Twitter bio.

BE SURE TO INCLUDE:

- ☐ Hudl link
- ☐ Height and weight
- ☐ High school and state
- ☐ GPA
- ☐ Test scores
- ☐ Position
- ☐ Graduation class
- ☐ Forty-yard dash time
- ☐ Phone number
- ☐ Twitter handle
- ☐ Email address
- ☐ YouTube link, if available

Put key specifics in the email's subject line: full name, graduation year, position, height, and weight. Send the email to your position-specific coach and the recruiting coordinator at each school. (It doesn't hurt to CC every coach on staff.)

Dear Coach Hart,

I am an athlete that excels in class and on the field. I am a powerhouse FB that continually finds the best possible decisions in every situation to better position my team for victory.

Hope to talk with you soon.

Name: Henry Junior

Phone number: (123)-456-7890

Email: h.junior@email.com

Twitter: https://twitter.com/juniorhenry123

Height: 6'3"

Weight: 180lbs

Grad Year: 2023

GPA: 3.7

High School: Playbook High School

My strengths: I'm a fast and agile FB with sturdy feet that makes hard to knock over. Fast decision maker and playmaker.

Links to Hudl film

In this example, the recruit does a great job of limiting words and getting to the important details. He's also getting an early start on promoting himself and has all of the stats and needed information readily available for coaches.

Fun Fact: Does this strategy work? Yes! I currently have a player in my position group that I recruited completely based off an initial email he sent me. He's from Texas, outside of my recruiting area. I happened to be looking for an edge rusher at the time, so I clicked on his Hudl film and liked what I saw. From there, I looked at his grades and stats. When they all checked out, I recruited him to come to our program, and I would not have if he had not initiated contact. He's here now, and he's thriving. Moral of the story: Are you hungry? Closed mouths don't get fed.

- **Spring:** Typically, a player's recruitment picks up tremendously after their junior football season. I recommend going to visit college campuses for:
  - Junior Day
  - Unofficial Visits

Attend both. However, as a word of advice, I am partial to unofficial visits over Junior Days for more individualized attention.

➔ **SCHEDULE AN END-OF-YEAR ACADEMIC MEETING WITH YOUR GUIDANCE COUNSELOR. (THIS ONE'S VERY IMPORTANT!)**

> **Memo:** As a junior heading into your senior year, by the end of this summer, you need to have ten core courses on your transcript (including seven in English, math, or science) before your seventh (fall of senior year) semester.
> *Very important: do not miss this!

At the end of the year (May/June), schedule a quick academic check-in with your guidance counselor and ask them to upload your transcript to the NCAA Eligibility Center.

Potential Early Enrollees (Greenshirts): Review the plan with your counselor to be sure you are still in position to graduate early (December of your senior year), if interested.

Finally, use this meeting to enroll in summer school options to replace or recover any and all Ds or Fs that are currently on your transcript for core classes. Remember, we want to replace them with As and Bs, *always!*

Pro Tip: Read this slowly—This is your *final* summer grade recovery/ replacement opportunity. Talk with your guidance counselor and check your transcript against your school's 48H form. Once you begin your seventh semester of high school (which is fall of your senior year), you may *not* repeat or replace any previous courses to improve your core-course GPA. Read that again!

➜ GO TO SUMMER FOOTBALL CAMPS.

If you are under-recruited at this point, use this time to showcase your talent during camps at your schools of choice.

Pro Tip: During camp, along with height and weight, coaches want to see how you compete, how you test, your body language, attitude, speed, level of coachability, forty-yard dash, agility (5-10-5), vertical jump, and performance during drills, as well as how you put forth maximum effort. These things and more are noticed and taken into account when schools give, on the spot, committable offers based on your performance at camp.

Coaches are evaluating whether or not:

- You are at the front of the line or lagging behind.
- You are able to accurately process the information given and finish drills.

Per the NCAA, once you begin your _____ semester of high school (which is fall of your senior year), you may **not** repeat or replace any previous courses to improve your core-course GPA. How can you replace low grades before then?

HUDDLE UP: SECTION REVIEW

☐   What key takeaways and new information have you learned
    in this chapter?

    _____

    _____

    _____

☐   What college camps do you think you should attend that
    would be the most beneficial for you?

    _____

    _____

    _____

☐   How many college football programs have you contacted and
    sent your Hudl film to?

    _____

    _____

    _____

☐   How important is this final grade check at the end of your
    junior year? Is there any recovery needed? What are your
    recovery strategies?

    _____

    _____

    _____

TIME-OUT:
OFFERS & COMMITMENTS

Enjoy the recruiting process, but keep in mind that football is a business. In the same manner that the school and football program choice you make can change your life, your choice affects the livelihood of your potential coach as well. Approach your recruitment with a business mindset.

According to the NCAA, about 22 percent of high school athletes nationwide are awarded some form of athletics scholarship to compete in college. If you are blessed to receive an offer, realize how truly fortunate you are, and be smart about the decision-making process.

Types of Offers (can vary by school)

- **Non-Committable Offer:** An expression of *interest* by the school. The program(s) will continue to watch the recruit. Non-committable offers *could* turn committable at a later time, should certain criteria be met and/or situations change.
- **Committable Offer:** A solid scholarship offer that prospects can accept and "cash in" at any time. As discussed earlier, FBS schools are only allowed to offer full scholarships. However, Division I-AA (FCS) and Division II schools are able to offer partial scholarships. For example, they can cover 25 percent of their college costs, leaving the student-athlete to cover the other 75 percent. These percentages can vary depending on what the coaches work out with the player.
- **Camp Offer:** In addition to the above, recruiting coaches will give what we call a camp offer.

WHAT IS A CAMP OFFER?

If presented a camp offer, it means that coaches are interested and like your film. But in order for your offer to become committable, you must first go to camp and perform live in front of the head coach to ensure them that your film matches up with your in-person performance.

As mentioned in "Time-Out: Know the Biz," FBS football programs are allowed to place eighty-five players at a time on scholarship, with a maximum of twenty-five of those spots allowed for first-year players. Because of that, many college programs end up in a position where they need more bodies than the twenty-five allowed for first-year players. This has given rise to grayshirt and blueshirt offers. *Here's where it becomes tricky!* Let's discuss:

- **Grayshirt Offer:** Prospects who are given grayshirt offers are sometimes referred to as "preferred walk-ons"—they are guaranteed a spot on the team and are going to receive all the support of normal scholarship athletes after their waiting period. A grayshirt is when a team offers a player enrollment on scholarship at the start of their second semester. Grayshirts enroll and go to class for the first semester as part-time students without starting their eligibility clocks. They are not on scholarship, cannot practice, and cannot play. After their semester waiting period, the athletes become full-time students and part of the team. Sometimes, grayshirt offers can turn into regular offers, and players can become regular signees due to surprise transfers and roster changes.
- **Blueshirt Offer:** The blueshirt rule allows schools to put athletes on scholarship at the start of practice as a freshman, but count them against the next year's scholarship total, as long as they don't "recruit" them and they don't play. Recruiting coaches can contact these prospects and have them on campus for unofficial visits, but the recruits must pay their own way. They are on scholarship, sign a NLI (a National Letter of Intent, which I will go over in the next chapter), can practice with the team, and can play.
- **Greenshirts:** These players will have a significant advantage over other incoming freshmen in their class because they will enroll at the school of their choice during the spring semester. This will allow them to go through spring football and start college courses. It provides them an early start from an academic and athletic standpoint.

Although not a part of the high school recruitment process, it
is also important to note what a "redshirt" is in college football.
According to the NCAA, every college athlete has five calendar
years to play four college seasons. In college football, if a player
doesn't participate in more than four games, then he is eligible for
a redshirt, which allows the player to use one year for development
(not counted toward his four years of play). Redshirts can be
valuable for a couple reasons. First, it will allow the player another
year of development and he will still have four years left to play.
This will also help the player get his bachelor's degree sooner
and potentially work toward a master's degree while the school
pays for it.

Here are the "shirt offers" that we have covered in the *Playbook*
at a glance:

Shirt offers	On scholarship?	Can play?	Can practice?
Grayshirt	No	No	No
Blueshirt	Yes	Yes	Yes
Greenshirt (early enrollees)	Yes	Yes	Yes

All clear? If you are entertaining multiple offers, congrats!
However, be honest in your communication with coaches to avoid
wasted time. Think of it like dating: if a coach is taking the time to
build and maintain a relationship with you, that shows interest and
potential for an offer.

Pro Tip: If a school has not offered you a scholarship, and you
currently have other offers, there are most likely still questions

about anything from your academics to your ranking on their recruiting board. There are many factors to be considered, and you are still being evaluated, so keep grinding in class and on the field!

> ### PARENT PRO TIP:
>
> Use this information on commitments and offers to help your player and better engage in the recruiting process.

Recruits, please understand that the recruiting process can become stressful for you. It is important to involve your loved ones because they can assist you in the decision-making process. Talk through these topics with them. Be wise about how you spend your time and money going on unofficial college visits. The goal here is to be efficient. Take visits where the interest has proven to be *mutual*.

How will you know?

- Typically, coaches will also engage parents in recruiting conversations when the interest is solid.
- Before visiting a campus, your recruit will have received a personal (and verbal) invitation to visit by the coach—not simply a Twitter direct message or a graphic sent.
- If coaches are in contact with you once or twice a week, they are interested. If it's sparingly—meaning once every couple of weeks—then they are not. You will know the difference.
- How quickly they respond to your call is also a sign. Usually if they are interested, they will respond the same day. If it takes them three days or more, that shows lack of interest.

Player's Note: Be able to hold a casual conversation with your recruiting coach. You could potentially spend the next phase (four years) of your life with them, so be sure to get acquainted.

SUGGESTED QUESTIONS TO ASK THE RECRUITING COACH:

☐ What are some fundamentals you teach the guys you coach?

☐ What are you looking for in student-athletes?

☐ Where am I on your recruiting board?

☐ What position would I be playing in your program?

☐ What football scheme is run on offense/defense?

Again, treat each conversation with a recruiting coach as an interview. Be mindful about how you communicate and the questions you ask because coaches are evaluating everything. It is okay to ask about the depth chart, just make sure you're coming from a place of not being concerned about competition, and that you're willing to work for a starting position.

ONCE YOU HAVE SECURED AN OFFER, TO BE 100 PERCENT CLEAR, ASK:

☐ What does my offer mean? (Is this a full-ride scholarship or partial?)

☐ Is my offer committable?

☐ What position am I being offered?

☐ Where do you see me fitting into your scheme?

☐ How many spots do you have in this recruiting class and at my position?

Pro Tip: If you have a committable offer in hand, I recommend committing the spring or summer before your senior year.

CONSIDER THIS WHEN CHOOSING YOUR COMMITMENT PICK:

☐ Does the school have your major?

☐ Have you and your parents visited the campus?

☐ Have you built a good rapport with the coaching staff?

☐ Have you have spoken to current players about the school and position coach?

☐ Have they run a scheme that you feel comfortable with and that fits your skill set?

☐ Do you and your parents feel comfortable with the decision to commit?

Why commit now? As aforementioned, a majority of players receive offers based on their junior season film. If by the end of the year, you have built a great relationship with the school's staff and can answer the points above in the affirmative, you should strongly consider committing to secure your scholarship. Some players choose to hold out and take a gamble on a bigger school or "better" offer, only to lose their spot due to unfortunate injury, change in circumstance, or another player choosing to "jump in the boat" ahead of them. Now don't get me wrong, holding out *does* work in the end for some. But also keep in mind that there are just as many tough losses as there are wins when it comes to the waiting game. Keep your goals at the forefront.

The Four Football Recruiting Periods

There are four recruiting periods set by the NCAA that recruits need to be aware of and college coaches must abide by:

- Contact Period
- Evaluation Period
- Quiet Period
- Dead Period

It is important for recruits and families to know that coaches are constantly working in one of these four recruiting periods each day of the year.

- **Contact Period:** First is the "contact period," when the recruiting flood gates are wide open! During the contact period, coaches can make in-person, face-to-face contact with recruits and their families up to three weeks prior to signing day. During this time, coaches make school visits, watch student-athletes compete at high school games, write and call recruits and their parents, and are also allowed to come to a recruit's home. My personal favorite home visits have been in New Orleans, Louisiana. I love a good home-cooked meal, and in my experience, their food is second to none. On one visit, a recruit's parent cooked chicken and sausage gumbo and homemade cracklins. I also remember that the head coach accompanying me on this particular visit took a few bites and proceeded to put the entire bag of cracklins into his pocket to take home. They were just that good!
- **Evaluation Period:** The next recruiting period is called the "evaluation period." The evaluation period allows coaches to write, call, and go and visit schools, practices, and games to speak with high school coaches and collect information on recruits. Coaches are not allowed to have face-to-face

contact with recruits or their parents during this period off the college's campus. The evaluation period occurs from late April through May. This is a big evaluation period for coaches because this time allows them to come and watch high school teams in spring practice. Many coaches use this period to visit track meets to watch multi-sport athletes as well.

- **Quiet Period:** The "quiet period" dictates the time during the recruitment process when coaches are not allowed to leave a college campus to visit high schools or have off-campus contact with players. Coaches may still write and call players and parents. This period is during the summer months when high school athletes attend summer prospect camps on college campuses.

  - Note: During the contact, evaluation, and quiet periods, recruits are allowed to visit college campuses to have face-to-face contact with college coaches. College coaches are restricted by NCAA rules as to when they can initiate contact or make phone calls to recruits. However, recruits may call coaches at any time. For specific dates, you can pull up the recruiting calendar on the NCAA website.

- **Dead Period:** The last recruiting period is the "dead period." The dead period prohibits coaches from initiating calls or having in-person contact with recruits. Coaches may continue to write players during any period. Although this seems extreme, it's beneficial for the recruits and coaches, as the dead period falls during winter break and fall camp. I think coaches and players need a break from the grind of recruiting. This is especially true during winter break, when most are unplugging and spending quality time with family, and during fall camp as every college team is locked in and preparing for their upcoming season.

Coaches can	Visit high school	Call	Write	Face-to-Face contact off-campus
Contact Period	Yes	Yes	Yes	Yes
Evaluation Period	Yes	Yes	Yes	No
Quiet Period	No	Yes	Yes	No
Dead Period	No	No	Yes	No

Re: The Injury Report

Let's discuss a serious "what if," and a potential "elephant in the *recruiting* room"—injuries. They suck, rehab isn't fun, and as an athlete, they're a common part of the dance.

Q: What if a player gets an injury during the recruiting process?

A: When you sustain an injury, first evaluate the extent of the injury. Is it an ankle sprain that will require a couple weeks of rehab, and you'll be back to normal? Or is it something more severe? If it's an injury as simple as an ankle sprain, then it's not a big deal. If it's an injury that is more severe such as a head, Achilles, ACL, or other injury that requires some type of surgery, you should notify the coaches who have extended offers and discuss the injury with them. Honesty is the best policy. Avoid dishonesty regarding your injury at all costs, as the coaches will eventually find out. The deception will potentially void your offer and put a serious damper on your relationships with recruiting coaches.

When discussing your injury, ask the coaches if your offer is committable or if the injury has changed your standing. If you still have a committable offer on the table, I would seriously consider securing it with your commitment.

If you sustained an injury as a junior and you are a guy who needed senior film to get offers due to slow recruitment, I recommend sending out junior film to schools with hopes that your most recent film will pique some interest and potentially score you an offer. Again, players should disclose injuries to recruiters. If there are no offers that come along, then reach out to junior colleges about going the JUCO route, or consider the walk-on option at your school of choice. FBS schools can only have a total of eighty-five players on scholarship at a time. They can have over one hundred players on the roster. These other twenty-five to thirty players are walk-ons. Walk-ons are players who decided to join the football program without a scholarship. They are fully funding their college education or may have academic scholarships to the college or university. This option can be utilized by players trying to continue their football playing career at the next level with no athletic scholarship offers.

Some players who have suffered significant injuries make the decision to reclassify (pushing their graduation date back) and stay in high school for an extra year to get healthy, go through spring ball (providing college coaches an opportunity to evaluate them during the spring), get game film from their final season in high school, and attend summer camps. This option can reenergize the recruitment process and garner fresh interest from coaches after an injury.

I recently had this injury experience recruiting a player and offered him a scholarship in the spring. He was high on the recruiting board and the coaching staff was really excited about him. He committed to our program in the late spring. During the third or fourth week of his senior football season, he sustained a foot injury that required surgery. This would make him miss the remainder of his senior season.

He was forthcoming with the coaching staff and let us know everything that happened. Although I was disappointed that he wasn't going to be able to finish his senior season with his teammates, I was encouraged by the fact that I was bringing a quality young man into the program. His being so forthcoming gave me a peek into his character and that was a big plus for me. Unfortunately, injuries occur with football, but based on where we are in modern medicine, people can recover really well from injuries. They no longer have to be a deal-breaker in many cases, especially for young players. For them, the recovery and bounce back is typically just as strong, if not stronger than before.

Final Thoughts: Injuries can be hard to navigate and are a discouraging part of the process, but overcoming adversity is the motto, so stay encouraged and find a way!

CONVERSATION STARTERS:

1. Explain the types of offers in your own words:
   - Non-Committable Offer
   - Committable Offer
   - Camp Offer
2. Explain the difference between a grayshirt and a blueshirt offer.
3. Why is your college choice such an important decision?
4. How should recruits handle reporting injuries?

HUDDLE UP: SECTION REVIEW

☐   What key takeaways and new information have you learned
    in this chapter?

    _____

    _____

    _____

    _____

☐   How has the information you've learned in this chapter made
    you rethink and reimagine what your life as a college player
    can look like?

    _____

    _____

    _____

    _____

CHAPTER 10

REDZONE—TWELFTH GRADE (X)

My twelfth grade year was very eye-opening. There was a player who was younger than me garnering a lot of attention from big-time schools. I felt like I was the better player, but he was picking up the SEC offers. He was around six feet, four inches, 230 pounds; I was five feet, eleven inches, 240 pounds. My grades were in the tank and he took care of his. Yes, this situation was a difficult pill to swallow for me and extremely frustrating, but going through this taught me to not be jealous of anyone else's journey and just run my own race.

I quickly realized that I was in a deep academic hole my senior year. I had no idea how to dig myself out of it, or if I even had the time left at this point to do so. I had not studied for it, but knew I needed to take the ACT, and based on my GPA, I knew that I needed to make at least an 18. I thought my GPA was okay, but I did not know what a core GPA was. I didn't score the 18. My recruitment was very slow, and for obvious reasons, I did not have many schools speaking to me at all. I had conversations with coaches from Rice, Southern Miss, Jackson State, and Delta State, none of which resulted in offers. The only school that offered me scholarship money was Holmes Community College in Mississippi, and that was a 50 percent scholarship offer. Man, that was a tough blow—or so I thought at the time. Please learn from my blind spots to put yourself in the most advantageous position possible. Let's dive into your grand finale!

GPS voice "You've arrived!" Your senior year somewhat seals the deal in our recruitment plan. This year, we will lock in the bounty of our successes and, same as before, we need to assess and redirect to overcome our challenges. The good news is that we have a solid plan to execute. The bad news is that we're knocking at graduation's door, and our time to execute our plan is dwindling quickly. Your senior year can be likened to the fourth quarter of a game. In football, we often talk about the importance of a strong finish and the mindset to always finish what you start.

"Leaving no stone unturned," let's take our final lap!

HERE'S THE PLAY:

☐ Read through the twelfth grade plan
☐ Prioritize your academics and focus on grades
☐ Schedule ACT/SAT retakes as needed
☐ Update your Hudl film and Twitter bio stats
☐ Sign your NLI
☐ Complete your college application and FASFA
☐ Schedule an end-of-year academic meeting
☐ Submit final updates and forms on your NCAA Eligibility Center account

➜ **PRIORITIZE YOUR ACADEMICS AND FOCUS ON GRADES!**

Grade Check: Meet with your counselor as early as possible (Summer/Fall). Check your current course registration to make sure you will graduate on time with sixteen core courses for NCAA eligibility.

HERE'S THE CHECKLIST:

☐ Four years of English

☐ Three years of math (Algebra 1 or higher)

☐ Two years of natural/physical science (including one year of lab science if your high school offers it)

☐ One additional year of English, math, or natural/ physical science

☐ Two years of social science

☐ Four additional years of English, math, natural/physical science, social science, foreign language, comparative religion, or philosophy

☐ Double-check (and triple-check) your transcript *and* your current class schedule! Are you on track?

Remember: You must have a minimum core GPA of 2.3 to be a full qualifier.

Check your test scores and core GPA against the Division I sliding scale to determine your needs. Do you need a higher core GPA, test score, or both?

➜ **RETAKE THE ACT OR SAT IF NEEDED.**

Pro Tip: Choose the testing format that you performed best on to retake! Submit your scores to the NCAA using code 9999.

- Not a great test taker? Get your core GPA as high as you possibly can and thank the heavens above for the Division I sliding scale.
- Once your results are received, check your SAT combined score or ACT sum score and match it with your core-course

GPA on the Division I sliding scale again. Use the sliding scale to know what numbers you need to hit.

- If you have a low test score, you need a higher core-course GPA to be eligible. If you have a low core-course GPA, you need a higher test score to be eligible.
- You have no more grade replacement or recovery options now, so hug a teacher! Do your absolute best in your current course enrollments. Meet with teachers, attend their study sessions, and seek extra help. Remember: teachers are your teammates. They are helping you get where you want to be.

➜ **"GET AFTER IT" AND ENJOY YOUR SENIOR YEAR OF FOOTBALL!**

Add your senior season highlights to your Hudl film. Update your bio and stats on Twitter. Remember to add your most explosive plays first. College coaches want to see the best plays in your most recent film.

> ### NOVEMBER OF YOUR SENIOR YEAR:
>
> Not being recruited at this point but still want to be around the game? Start making contact now to work the team and potentially earn scholarship money off the field. Find the details in chapter 11.

➜ **SIGN YOUR NLI AND LOCK IN YOUR SCHOLARSHIP.**

Take official visits and sign your National Letter of Intent (NLI) on "Signing Day" in December or February.

WHAT IS A NATIONAL LETTER OF INTENT (NLI)?

An NLI is signed by a college-bound student-athlete as an agreement to attend a Division I or II college or university for one academic year. Signing an NLI ends the recruiting process since schools are prohibited from recruiting student-athletes who have already signed letters with other schools. If a student signs an NLI with one school but attends a different school, they will lose one full year of eligibility and must complete a full academic year at their new school before being eligible to compete in sports.

Pro Tip: I recommend signing on the December signing day to lock in your scholarship. Keep in mind that every team in America has a limited number of scholarships, and your spot may be filled by another athlete (with a committable offer) and be unavailable for you in February.

- Due to the new early signing period, coaching staffs across the country aim to be done with 90 to 95 percent of their recruiting class in December, so keep that in mind.
- After December, coaches typically use the spring to get an early jump on the next recruiting class. Don't miss out!

Pro Tip: Once you've signed, it is a great idea to ask your position coach to send you a digital copy of the playbook, if possible. This will give you an early start on learning your position, which can help you get on the field sooner.

→ **COMPLETE YOUR COLLEGE APPLICATION AND FASFA.**

Once the NLI is signed and filed, your scholarship is officially locked in. At this point, most players complete their college admissions application (if they didn't already when they committed). The athletics and admissions departments work together closely, so student-athlete applications are expedited and processed quickly.

Also, complete your Federal Student Aid (FAFSA®) for the upcoming summer session of college and the following fall. Be sure to complete both (two separate applications and subsequent years) at the same time, and prior to arriving on campus (i.e., complete FAFSA 2020–2021 and 2021–2022). Don't overlook this step as you can potentially receive free federal aid based on your parents' income. *#winning*

→ **SCHEDULE AN END-OF-YEAR ACADEMIC MEETING.**

☐ Complete all academic and amateurism questions in your NCAA Eligibility Center account.

☐ Request your final amateurism certification beginning April 1 for fall college enrollees.

After you graduate, ask your counselor to submit your final official transcript with proof of graduation to the NCAA Eligibility Center. Again, show your appreciation by sending your counselor a handwritten thank-you letter—it's part of being a good teammate!

EXTENSION ACTIVITY: #GIVETHANKS TO YOUR "TEAM"

The Task: As discussed in the *Playbook*, no one gets anywhere alone. Students will create thank-you notes or notes of appreciation to share with members of their "team." Create five different notes with messages for five individuals at school or in the community. You may choose fellow students, family, mentors, or school faculty and staff members. These are your "VIPs," so write at least four to five sentences giving each individual a personal message of thanks for encouraging you, helping you reach your goals, and being a part of your "team."

Supplies: notebook, construction or unlined paper, and art supplies

CONVERSATION STARTERS:

1. Have you narrowed down the list of schools you would like to attend? What are your top three schools?
2. If recruiting is slow, what options are available?
3. What factors will matter most in narrowing down your top choice?

Let's Debate: Should players have to have a higher GPA to qualify for the NCAA than they do to graduate from high school?

HUDDLE UP: SECTION REVIEW

☐ What key takeaways and new information have you learned
in this chapter?

_____

_____

_____

_____

☐ Now that you've experienced the four-year planning
process, how will you continue the practice of planning your
athletic career?

_____

_____

_____

_____

Part III

POST-GAME /
OVERTIME—O

CHAPTER 11

NEXT PLAY (X)

It's been a long trek, but you made it to the other side. If you executed *The Recruit's Playbook* properly with no shortcuts, you are no longer a high school athlete. Congratulations! You're in preparation to embark on the next phase of your life's journey as a collegiate athlete.

Next Step: Pay it forward and pass this playbook on to the next recruit. Still have some loose ends to tie up? *That's okay, keep reading.*

•••

Move on to the next play. You've got decisions to make. To the non-qualifier who still has the desire to play at the next level: there are other options for you. Your dreams are not dead. You will simply need to take a different route, as I did. That's all. You cannot change the past, so learn from your mistakes, make adjustments based on your circumstances, and overcome adversity. Let's build from here and persevere. Start the process by assessing your situation. Do you have the sixteen core courses required, but not the 2.3 core GPA? You can still potentially redshirt at your college of choice. You can also look into college preparatory schools and junior colleges that offer football.

To the qualifier, but not highly recruited athlete: you have more options after high school as well. In addition to the options above, you can look into the walk-on process at the school of your choice.

There is an opportunity to showcase your talent, compete for a roster spot, potentially get on scholarship, and keep pursuing your dream of playing college football. Keep in mind that the walk-on process can be difficult, so research the depth chart and choose the school wisely.

Pro Tip: Do your research and consider schools that are not loaded in depth at your position to increase your chances of making the roster.

Take an honest assessment of your situation. If after exhausting all of your resources, it looks as though competing athletically after high school is not an option for you, there are still more opportunities and potential to earn scholarship money off the field. You can continue to have access to the game you love and enjoy the perks of traveling with the team, attending events, free meals, free athletic gear, on-the-job training, and networking with the athletics department and team staff. As mentioned during your senior year, around November, if this option is appealing, you should apply for college acceptance and start contacting schools to make your interest known.

EVERY COLLEGE FOOTBALL PROGRAM (AND ALL ATHLETICS FOR THAT MATTER) AT EVERY LEVEL HAS STUDENT POSITIONS ON AND OFF THE FIELD, SUCH AS:

- Video/digital assistants
- Equipment managers
- Undergraduate assistants
- Recruiting assistants/interns
- Athletic training assistants

These positions often come with scholarship money attached, and some even offer full rides depending on the level of the division. Also, these positions can turn into a long-term career off the field. These positions can offer a salary and health insurance. So here's the *how-to*. Once your college application has been accepted, do your research and reach out to the Director of Football Operations (DFO) and the Director of Player Personnel (DPP) at your college(s) of choice. Draft a quick email to each of them (separately) inquiring about the availability of student positions and working with the team for the upcoming year. *It doesn't hurt to also attach a résumé.* Here's a sample email:

To: [Insert DFO or DPP email address]

Subject: Inquiry: Student Position w/ team Fall 2023

Dear DFO [insert name],

My name is John Smith and I'm an incoming freshman. I work hard, I love the game of football, and would greatly appreciate an opportunity to assist the team next year if there are any student positions available.

I am arriving on campus this summer, and I'm readily available to assist with on- and off-the-field tasks as needed. If interested, please contact me at [insert email] and [insert phone number]. My résumé is also attached.

Thank you for your time and consideration. Go Dawgs!

—John

If you don't hear back, be sure to follow up with a phone call and leave a message. If you are open to attending any college, sometimes you can find these positions posted on sports blogs such as FootballScoop.com.

So again, remember that you've got options. Things may not go as you pictured or planned, but detours still get you to the destination. No matter what, keep pushing. This is simply a plot twist!

As a coach, I encourage my players to grow comfortable with being uncomfortable. This is a skillset that will benefit you for the rest of your life.

> "WHOEVER PLAYS THE HARDEST, THE LONGEST, USUALLY WINS THE GAME."
> —TOM MOORE

Need more context as to what that looks like? Read my story in the next chapter.

EXTENSION ACTIVITY: RÉSUMÉ WRITING (COLLEGE & CAREER READINESS)

Résumé writing is a valuable skill that will be beneficial for athletes and individuals working alongside the team in an off-the-field role. Generally speaking, at some point in life, everyone will need a résumé. This can be used for internships, volunteer work, or simply applying for a job.

The Task: As a tie-in to your career education program, and as mentioned in the "Separate Yourself" and "Next Play" chapters of the *Playbook*, résumés come in handy. Have each student format and create a résumé. The students should be sure to include in the résumé a statement of their goals and a detailed account of their experience, work history (if applicable), and interests.

Supplies: paper, writing utensil, word processor/résumé template, computer

Extension: As mentioned in this chapter, there are many potential careers off the field that players can pursue. Research and report on alternate career options for football lovers and what skills should be listed on their résumés (e.g., Tech: Video Game Designer).

Link to media: www.pbslearningmedia.org/resource/ a16b6e70-01cc-4fb0-9905-26daea72c8fe/a16b6e70-01cc-4fb0-9905-26daea72c8fe

CONVERSATION STARTERS:

1. What are your options to play at the next level if you don't qualify or have not secured a scholarship by your high school graduation date?
2. "Whoever plays the hardest, the longest, usually wins the game." Aside from the literal game reference, how can this quote be applied to the game of life? What does it mean?

HUDDLE UP: SECTION REVIEW

☐ What key takeaways and new information have you learned
in this chapter?

_____

_____

_____

☐ How confident do you feel about the execution of your
recruitment plan?

_____

_____

_____

☐ In hindsight, what blind spots did you notice, if any?

_____

_____

_____

☐ What recommendations or advice would you have for
future high school student-athletes embarking on the
recruitment journey?

_____

_____

_____

CHAPTER 12

NO EXCUSES (O)

> "IF YOU REALLY WANT TO DO IT, YOU DO IT.
> THERE ARE NO EXCUSES."
> —BRUCE NAUMAN

Did I follow *The Recruit's Playbook*? Absolutely not. There wasn't one written for me to follow. I am no stranger to overcoming adversity and moving on to the next play. In sharing my story, I hope to encourage others along the way.

Brief history: I failed fourth and fifth grade—*major shout-outs to summer school*. In fact, my grades were average to below average all throughout grade school. I began my football journey in the seventh grade. Football gave me structure, stability, and a brotherhood. There is no doubt that football gave me something to hang my hat on and a sense of belonging. It allowed me to be a part of something that was bigger than myself. I was a non-qualifier out of high school and made a 16 on the ACT. As a matter of fact, I never studied for it and only took the ACT once, three months prior to my graduation date. At every step of my journey, I got stronger and wiser.

Encouraged yet? Wait, there's more—to add insult to injury, the only college football offer I had was a half scholarship to Holmes Community College in Mississippi. *Thank God for JUCO, Go Dawgs!* While I was in junior college, I took extra classes in the summer in order to graduate from Holmes in December. That decision enabled me to be an early enrollee and attend Central Arkansas in the spring semester.

Now's when we get to the good part. When faced with humbling situations in life, I learned the valuable lesson of finding comfort in the midst of my discomfort and grew to appreciate the difficult times. What I saw as stumbling blocks actually turned into stepping-stones in more ways than one. Today, I hold both a bachelor's and a master's degree. I received a key to the city from the mayor of Conway, Arkansas, where I completed my undergraduate degree after leaving Holmes. While attending the University of Central Arkansas, I was a two-time Conference Defensive Player of the Year and a two-time All-American. I was also selected to the All-Decades Team and currently hold the record for highest NFL draft pick in UCA's history, with the 5th round, 143rd overall pick in 2010.

In full view of my highs and lows, I would encourage anyone to simply keep pushing and never give up. Often in life, it's not the smartest people who make it. Instead, it's those who refuse to quit.

"TOUGH TIMES DON'T LAST. TOUGH PEOPLE DO."
—ROBERT SCHULLER

CONVERSATION STARTERS:

1. In this chapter, I discuss the importance of overcoming adversity to attain one's goals. Give examples from my personal story when I show how I did that. What can you relate to in my personal narrative? Discuss how my story is similar to yours, what you've learned, and how you can apply these ideas to your life. What are the major takeaways you see here?

2. *Don't @ Me:* Choose a question below to research. Then use your research to debate, write an argumentative essay, or persuasive speech.

   - Is participation in high school athletics worth it? What are the pros/cons?
   - Should colleges be held responsible for their athletes' mistakes?
   - Should college athletes be paid?
   - Should athletes be considered role models? Should character matter?
   - Should every Little League athlete get a participation trophy?
   - Do competitive sports overwhelm childhood or enhance it?
   - Should home-schoolers be allowed to play for high school teams?
   - Should girls be allowed to play tackle football?
   - Are racism and bullying present in football?
   - Does football promote aggression?
   - Are sports stars overpaid?
   - Should women be allowed to compete against men in football?

- Are college entrance exams fair?
- Should athletes be allowed to use school vouchers to play sports at private schools?

POST-READING QUESTIONS

Now that you have finished *The Recruit's Playbook*, review the notes and answers you've given along the way and answer the questions below. While answering, think about whether any of your thoughts or answers have changed since reading the *Playbook*.

- Why is it important to have a set plan and take an active role in the steps to attain one's goals?
- In *The Recruit's Playbook*, I factor in missteps and the need to make corrections. Why is this important?
- Are the decisions you've made helping or hurting your future goals? How do you course correct?
- Review how you planned to achieve your goals prior to reading the *Playbook*. Have the steps you planned changed, or can you edit and make them more specific now?
- Based on the information provided in *The Recruit's Playbook*, are you academically on track to be an NCAA qualifier? What are your areas of concern and what changes need to be made?
- What have been the best aspects and most challenging aspects of your recruitment process thus far? What advice would you give a younger student-athlete?
- Based on the information provided in the *Playbook*, how can you make improvements as a student-athlete?
- Which of the quotes in the *Playbook* stood out to you personally and had the most meaning? Why?
- What were your biggest surprises or misconceptions prior to reading *The Recruit's Playbook*?

POST-READING ACTIVITIES

Choose activities from the list below to follow up on your reading and test your knowledge.

1. Dear Author

The Task: After reading the book, students can write to me via the publisher (who always forwards emails and letters) or contact me directly at coachlarryhart@gmail.com. Students may ask questions or share thoughts. Include all elements of a friendly letter (date, greeting, body, closing, and signature).

Supplies: paper, pencil, envelope, self-addressed envelope, stamp, computer

Directions: Make sure you include your school address in the letter or include an envelope with your return address and the author's address. (Check the back of the book or author's website for the address. You may also send the letter directly to the address of the publisher, which should be on the copyright page of the book.)

2. Interview the Author

The Task: Students reading *The Recruit's Playbook* will work together (pairs or small groups) to create interview questions. Each student will come up with five questions to ask. The teacher will approve each student's questions. Once all questions are approved, students will work together to create a short interview video of themselves asking the questions and email it to the author.

Supplies: paper, writing utensils, video creation technology, app, or computer

3. Create Your Own Test

The Task: Students will create their own fifteen-question test about the text that could be given to other readers to check their understanding of the story and provide an answer key. This allows students to simultaneously think about the story and prepare for a final assessment. The test should include a combination of matching, multiple choice, true/false, short answer, essay questions, and a five-word minimum vocabulary section.

Supplies: writing utensils, paper

Extension: After the instructor has approved the tests, allow students to pair up and swap tests. Each student grades their partner (and maybe a portion of the grade counts).

4. News (Sports) Broadcast, Podcast, Book Trailer, or Quick "Scouting Report"

The Task: Time to create! News (sports) broadcasts, podcasts, and book trailers are much more sophisticated and time consuming, but they make for great culminating tasks in the content classroom.

Option 1: Sports Broadcast, Trailer, or "Scouting Report." Be sure to include title, author, publication date, ten facts you learned from the book, your favorite part of the book with an explanation of why it's your favorite, a four-to-five-sentence book review paragraph, and a visual of your book, complete with a one-to five-star rating and why.

Option 2: Podcast or Commercial. Set up a video station (i.e., class iPad) in the back of the classroom, provide brief instruction on how to use it (post an info sheet of simple instructions for reinforcement), and have each student video themselves presenting a thirty-second commercial. In the first thirty seconds of the commercial, students should tell what they liked about the book. The next minute (podcast-style) will feature the student reading a favorite line or blurb from the book—students should select a passage that might motivate others to want to read the book and discuss it. Choose an option and ask students to share their book knowledge in this engaging, tech/digital-inclusive format.

Supplies: video (smartphone, app, computer) creation technology

Extension: Students will present broadcast or trailer to classmates and answer follow-up questions based on a speaking and listening standards presentation rubric. Teachers should email it to parents so they can view their child's work.

5. Playbook Trivia!

The Task: Students create a *Jeopardy!*-style game based on the information presented in *The Recruit's Playbook*. This *Jeopardy!*-style reading review game is a fun way to do test prep and revisit information in nonfiction. This could be done with index cards and someone giving the answer, with student contestants vying to provide the correct question, or by creating an informational "bingo" game.

Supplies: game board printout (students could draw this component or do it digitally), writing paper, art supplies, writing utensils, computer

6. Sell It (Persuasive Writing)

The Task: Readers pretend to be a publicist for *The Recruit's Playbook*. The student writes and then delivers a sixty-second speech that will persuade other students to should read the book. Writing and speaking is the goal.

Supplies: paper, writing utensils

ACKNOWLEDGEMENTS

Having an idea and turning it into a book is as hard as it sounds, and more rewarding than I could have ever imagined. With that, I have many thanks to give.

I have to start by thanking God, without whom I am nothing.

To my awesome wife, Juliet: from querying, pitching, prompting, questioning, reading early drafts, and editing with your "red pen" (and passing it off to my beloved mother-in-law when your eyes were too crossed to go on), to giving me solicited and unsolicited advice (accompanied by the occasional hard eye-roll) on everything attached to this book spine, *The Recruit's Playbook* would not be a thing without you. You are everything and everything is you. Thank you for being my #1 and my best recruit of all time.

Many thanks to my fantastic agent, Jessica, my amazing editors, MJ, Nate, and Yaddyra, and everyone on the Mango team for your insight, guidance, and (as a man of few words) pulling more out of me and onto these pages than I ever thought possible. I appreciate you taking a chance on me as a first-time author.

To my former teammate and friend, Rashad Jennings, for answering the call and penning a foreword like no other. I am truly grateful, brother.

Finally, to my wonderful family and all the coaches, teammates, and players who I have had the opportunity to lead and be led and inspired by over the years, I want to express my sincere gratitude for being the inspiration and the foundation for *The Recruit's Playbook*.

Your support means so much to me. Thank you!

ABOUT THE AUTHOR

Larry Hart is a Division I college football coach and Defensive Consultant at the University of Houston, and author of his book debut, *The Recruit's Playbook: A 4-Year Guide to College Football Recruitment for High School Athletes*. A native Mississippian, Coach Hart is steeped in football and applies his skillset as an enthusiast, All-American college athlete, alumni NFL draft pick, and current outside linebackers coach. With over a decade of firsthand knowledge of football athletics, Coach Hart has an experienced voice that efficiently guides readers and equips them with the tools and practical tips they need to succeed. Coach Hart has a master's degree in Communication Studies. He lives in Houston, Texas, with his wife, Juliet, and dreams of making his mark as a part-time, bestselling author.

CONNECT WITH COACH HART:

f CoachLarryHart

𝕏 @CoachLarryHart

◎ @coachlarryhart

www.coachlarryhart.com

Printed in the USA
CPSIA information can be obtained
at www.ICGtesting.com
JSHW082211140824
68134JS00014B/556